CANADA, EUROPE, AND HITLER

Canada, Europe, and Hitler

BY

WATSON KIRKCONNELL

M.A., Ph.D., F.R.S.C.

UNIVERSITY OF MANITOBA, WINNIPEG

TORONTO

OXFORD UNIVERSITY PRESS

1939

3678991

PRINTED IN CANADA
BY THE HUNTER-ROSE CO. LIMITED, TORONTO

PREFACE

The purpose of the present volume is to clarify some of the issues, both national and international, that confront Canada in the present war.

The manuscript began as an analysis of the opinions, with regard to Herr Hitler's policies and programme, of the two and a half million European-Canadians whose origin was neither British nor French. To this was prefixed a survey of the more recent developments in Central and Eastern Europe, and an estimate of the attitudes towards German expansion of the various European states, some of whose former nationals (or their descendants) are now citizens of the Dominion.

The tempo of international events has made necessary a drastic recasting of this material. German expansionists, whose bloodless occupation of Austria, Sudetenland, and Bohemia-Moravia had been dismissed by many as mere successful bluff, have shown themselves resolute and ruthless in devouring Poland; and France and Britain, with whom Canada is now associated, are engaged in a grim struggle to defeat the carnivorous nationalism of the Third Reich. Russian action has likewise altered the European picture fundamentally. For a Canadian, it thus becomes important to assess the issues at stake, both for the future of civilization and for the future of Canada.

Facts and opinions set forth in Part I ("Europe Faces Hitler") are derived in considerable measure from extensive European travel, especially visits in 1938 in Germany, Czechoslovakia, former Austria, Italy, Jugoslavia, Hungary, Rumania, Poland, Freistadt Danzig, East Prussia, Lithuania, Latvia, Estonia, Finland, Sweden, Norway,

v

and Denmark. Printed source material is indicated in the partial bibliography at the end of the volume.

The analysis of European-Canadian opinion in Part II grows out of a rather extensive contact with the vernacular press of the various European groups in Canada. For several years past I have been contributing to the *University of Toronto Quarterly* an annual survey of "New-Canadian Letters", which has involved my regular reading of most of the foreign-language newspapers in the Dominion. For the purposes of the present volume, I have thrown my net a little farther, so as to include all of these papers without exception (some forty periodicals in fourteen languages), and I have been clipping long and extensively from their editorial columns. The initial responsibility for this selection of material must rest with myself. To expedite, however, the final sifting of my unwieldy mass of data and the translation of relevant excerpts, I have availed myself of the collaboration of Mr. Honoré Ewach for the Slavic press, Mr. Edward Parker for the Jewish press, and Mr. B. W. Sabelli for the Finnish press. In the case of the other language-groups (German, Dutch, Danish, Norwegian, Swedish, Icelandic, Italian, and Magyar), the final distillation is my own. Responsibility for the analysis of opinion in all the groups also rests with me. Such an analysis can, of course, only be approximate, for all the subscribers to any newspaper do not necessarily support its political views; yet there must be a fair measure of such support or else the paper could not survive.

Contributory to my analysis has been the experience of three years (1916-19) as an officer under the Federal Department of Justice in the handling of interned aliens in Canada during the Great War.

United College,
October, 1939. WATSON KIRKCONNELL

CONTENTS

vii

PART ONE

EUROPE FACES HITLER

CHAPTER I

WHY BRITAIN IS AT WAR

HUMAN civilization faces today one of its greatest crises in all history. Out of the morass of post-War weakness, poverty, and irresolution there has arisen to sinister eminence a great man of action, as fanatical as Mahomet and as ruthless as Tamerlane. Adolf Hitler has made it plain from the very outset of his political career that his aim is world empire for Germany. Realizing that such an ideal could not be achieved without war, he not only prepared to forge the German nation into the greatest military machine of all time but was resolute enough to reveal to the nation, in his book *Mein Kampf*, that beyond all the inevitable hardship and sacrifice lay a culminating destiny. So candid in its brutality, violence, and cunning was this "political testament" of the Fuehrer, that the majority of those few Anglo-Saxons who could read this otherwise elusive book in the original German tended to dismiss its programme as too fantastic to be taken seriously. Its progressive fulfilment, however, from successful rearmament down to the pitiless obliteration of Poland, has compelled all men to realize that the nightmare of *Mein Kampf* is being implacably transmuted into reality and that democratic nations must defend themselves against a threat to world liberty.

His spurious and dangerous doctrines of race and living space will be dealt with below, in Chapters II and III respectively. It will suffice here to indicate briefly the character of his world programme in its "continental" and "oceanic" phases. The former involves the subjection of Europe, especially the U.S.S.R., and the co-ordination of all these resources in upbuilding a vast industrial state compared with which either Britain or the United States would be a pygmy in strength. Germany, in command of Russian iron, coal, and petroleum, could utterly outbuild the fleets and armaments of any other country. Granted this colossal consolidation at the European home base, Hitler could then proceed to that "oceanic" or global domination without which the Nazis cannot be satisfied; and a Pax Germanica would at last hold a fretful world in awe. Speaking of the need for national unity in such an endeavour, Hitler says:

If, in its historical development, the German people had possessed the same herd-unity that has stood other peoples in good stead, the German Empire would today be master of the globe. History would have taken another course, and who can say if this course would not have led to what so many purblind pacifists hope to get by whining and whimpering—a peace, not supported by the tearful pacifist lamentations of palm-waving females, but founded upon the victorious sword of a ruling race bending the world to the service of a higher culture? (*Mein Kampf*, 311th German edition, Munich, 1938, pp. 437-8).

The régime established itself in Germany, not by the will of the German people, but by terrorism and propaganda. In its very essence it calls for a ruthless extinction of every rival creed, whether civil or religious. Hitler himself, in defending and glorying in this intolerance, proclaims National Socialism as an infallible Faith that will permit no rivals to survive:

Christianity likewise could not be satisfied with building its own altar, but had of necessity to proceed to the destruction of the heathen altars. Only from this fanatical intolerance could a belief beyond contradiction come; this intolerance is even an absolute prerequisite for it. A faith filled with infernal intolerance can be broken only by a pure and genuinely new idea, driven forward by the same spirit of intolerance and fighting with the same invincible will. One may today acknowledge with sorrow that in the much freer world of antiquity the first Terror of the spirit came with the appearance of Christianity; but one cannot deny the fact that since then the world has been ruled and driven by this compulsion, and that force can only be broken by force and terror by terror. Only then can a new order be built up and created. Political parties are inclined to compromise, faiths never. Political parties take opponents into account; faiths proclaim their infallibility. (*Mein Kampf*, pp. 506-7).

In advancing this unholy Faith, no means are too cruel or too unscrupulous. Early in *Mein Kampf* (pp. 252-3), Hitler stresses the importance of lying, especially the use of such gross, mouth-filling lies as will carry conviction by their very effrontery. He also explains the technique of vilification and violence (*Mein Kampf*, p. 46 *et seq.*) whereby a blameless opponent can be unnerved and overwhelmed. Neither is there the slightest mercy for the vanquished. As the Czechs have learned since the surrender of March 1939, kicking a man when he is down is to Nazi mentality the very thing you knocked him down for. In a world dominated by Naziism, all men of independent thought could only expect flogging and death in concentration camps.

Realization that a frontal attack on the whole world is premature, and that possible foes ought to be defeated singly, Hitler's world programme calls for such revolutionary penetration as will set up in all susceptible countries Nazi governments, favourable to Germany in temperament and policy. Even more than Communism, Naziism is today a force seeking to dominate the world through revolution—whether it be controlling Belgium by the Flemish Nationalist Movement, Brazil by the Integralist Movement, Hungary by the "Arrow Cross" group, or

Canada by the National Unity Party. No movement of
our time has revealed a comparable demonic energy in
penetrating and organizing all possible communities the
world over, with a view to establishing the ultimate world
supremacy of Hitler's Reich.

The symbol of the Nazi world revolution is the concentration camp, the living grave of civil and religious liberty.
Dachau and Sachsenhausen and Oranienburg, with their
torture-chambers and their sadistic SA and SS guards and
their bloody motto of "Blut muss fliessen" (Blood must
flow) are grim monuments of tyranny, compared with
which the Bastille of long ago was a mere village gaol. In
like spirit, the whole unhappy country, even in peacetime,
has been honeycombed with secret police and informers
and even radio spies (*Funkwarte*) in every street and
apartment block, to make sure that no one listens to programmes from outside Germany. The enmity towards
religion is as explicit as that against civil liberty and its
expression ranges from foul trumped-up trials of the clergy
to the wholesale paganizing of the younger generation.
The marching song of the 12,000,000 lads in the Hitler
Jugend—"Christus krepiere, Hitler Jugend marschiere!",
i.e. "Let Christ rot and the Hitler Youth go marching on!"
—is a typical revelation of the Nazi attack on the Christian faith in Germany.

Against this whole evil movement, which bestraddles
prostrate Germany, Austria, Czechoslovakia, and Poland,
and breathes out threatenings and slaughter towards the
rest of the world, Britain and the British Commonwealth
are now at war. For six years, lie after gigantic lie and
aggression after brutal aggression have kept Europe in a
state of panic and confusion. It would be possible, in
melancholy retrospect, to see the extent to which disunity,

stupidity, and downright weakness on the part of Hitler's potential enemies have contributed to his success. Re-armament, the occupation of the Rhineland, intervention in Spain, and the seizure of Austria were watched with lack-lustre eyes. The major crisis of Munich found France disunited and Britain relatively unarmed; and many, including Mr. Chamberlain, felt that Hitler was sincere in citing the Sudetenland as "the last territorial claim that I have to make in Europe". With the occupation of Bohemia-Moravia on the Ides of March, 1939, the utter falseness of the Fuehrer at last became obvious, even to the most naïve. Thereafter none could doubt that the whole arrogant programme of *Mein Kampf* constituted the blue-prints for a deliberate subjugation of the world's liberty. Startled into sudden earnestness by the gathering storm, Britain hastened to give her guarantee of protection to countries like Poland, Rumania, and Greece, that lay in the path of Nazi aggression. A German demand for Danzig, designed to strangle Poland economically in order to dismember her at leisure, passed swiftly into demands for Poznania and the Corridor, and thence into a swift and merciless attack that has reduced the great city of Warsaw to fifty square miles of blood-spattered wreckage and placed the heroic Polish nation under a brutal yoke.

The British case for war is simple and inspiring: Hitler has proven himself a savage tyrant whose insatiable ambition will not stop short of world domination. He has broken every promise he has ever made—except his promise to be implacable in destroying his enemies. To make peace with such a man is to ensure crisis after crisis, as he seeks to impose his will on the world. The only hope of saving the freedom of the nations of Europe is to overthrow Hitler and the whole Nazi system associated

with him. The Poles and Czechs must be restored to free
nationhood. The Nazi demon must be exorcised from the
body of the luckless German nation. The alternative is
the rule of that demon throughout the world. If Britain
and France were defeated and their fleets and air forces
added to those of the Reich, even the United States would
be outnumbered fifteen to one and her defenders could be
blasted from the sea and the air. In a very real sense, the
Franco-British war against Nazidom is a war for world
freedom.

There is a second side to the declared policy of Britain,
a side as important as the first. A clear distinction has
been drawn between the German nation and the Nazi
incubus that bedevils it and chokes its liberties. Britain
seeks to save not only the world but Germany itself from
Hitler and Naziism. If these evil Things can once be
destroyed, Britain promises that she is ready to co-operate
with a free and democratic Germany in the upbuilding of
a new European order. In such a co-operative effort,
colonies, living space, raw materials, and a more effective
system of international peace, perhaps even some degree
of European federation, could be considered. The states-
men of Britain, in their wisdom, realize not merely that a
war explicitly to destroy or cripple German nationhood
would so unite that great people in a frenzy of resistance
that we might well lose the war, but also that without the
explicit ideal of ultimate peacetime collaboration with a
liberated German nation, our war-time passions would
issue in a vindictive peace settlement that would again
sow dragon's teeth for our children. Difficult as it may
sometimes seem, we must, as our highest patriotic duty,
keep it clear to ourselves and our neighbours that we are
not fighting against the German nation, German music,

German literature, and all of the German legacy to our joint civilization. The great German nation must be assured of a just and major part in any permanent settlement of Europe and the world. The character, endowments, and education of its people, coupled with their military and industrial formidability, renders ephemeral any peace that denies them their due share in the privileges and responsibilities of a co-operative world. Their citizens, moreover, by their qualities of mind and heart, are, for an Anglo-Canadian, perhaps the most immediately congenial of all Europeans. The present tragic conflict is not directed against our Germanic kindred but against the aggressive menace of Nazidom.

CHAPTER II

NAZI RACIAL DOGMA

THE cornerstone of Hitler's ideology is a passionate belief in the racial superiority of the German people over all other existing human stocks and its consequent duty, *sub specie aeternitatis*, to assure by its survival the preservation of that supreme human culture that is entrusted to it alone. A few quotations from *Mein Kampf* will make this point clear:

All that we admire today on this earth—learning and art, science and invention—is the creative product of only a few nations and perhaps originally of *one* race. On it depends the survival of all this culture. If it collapses, all the beauty of this earth sinks with it into the grave. (*Mein Kampf*, 311th edition, Munich, 1938, p. 316).

What we behold today of human culture, and of the results of art, learning, and science, is almost exclusively the creative product of the Aryan. But this fact permits the not-unwarranted conclusion that it is only the founder of higher civilization, and hence its prototype, that we understand by the word "man". He is the Prometheus of humankind, from whose bright forehead shone the divine spark of genius for all time. (*Ibid.*, p. 317).

The man who realizes but disregards the law of race brings upon himself indeed the fate that seems ordained for him. He hinders the triumphal march of the best race and thereby the prerequisite for all human progress. As a consequence, he reduces himself, while laden with the sensitivity of mankind, to the range of the helpless beast. (*Ibid.*, p. 317).

Thus the road that the Aryan has had to tread has been clearly indicated. As a conqueror he has overwhelmed inferior races and then ruled their practical activities by his command, according to his will, and for his own aims. In directing them into useful, though also laborious activities, he not only protected the lives of the conquered but also gave them a lot that was better than their former so-called "liberty". So long as he arbitrarily maintained his position as master, he remained in truth not only their lord but the sustainer and extender of civilization. (*Ibid.*, p. 324).

What we have to fight for is the assurance of the stability and increase of our race and our nation, the nurture of our children, the preservation of the purity of our blood, and the freedom and independence of the Fatherland, in order that our nation may bring to fulfilment the mission bestowed on it by the Creator of the Universe. (*Ibid.*, p. 234).

It (the National Socialist movement) must remain aware that we, as guardians of the highest civilization on this earth, are obligated to a supreme duty, and it will be able to measure up better to this duty the more it takes care that the German nation succeeds racially in recollecting it, and has pity on its own blood, apart from the herd of dogs, horses, and cats. (*Ibid.*, p. 732).

He who speaks of the Mission of the German nation on earth must realize that it can exist only in the creation of a state that sees its highest task in the preservation and extension of the inviolate and most noble ingredient of our nationality, the noblest of all mankind. By this the state receives for the first time a high spiritual aim. Over against the ridiculous task of the securing of peace and law (in order peacefully to facilitate mutual chicanery), there appears as a truly high mission the preservation and furtherance of the highest human race bestowed on this earth by the kindness of the Almighty. Instead of the dead mechanism of a state that exists only for its own sake, there must be formed a living organism with the express purpose of serving a higher ideal: The German Reich must, as a state, include all Germans, with the purpose not only of gathering and preserving all the nation's most precious primordial elements but of leading them slowly and surely on to a position of world domination. (*Ibid.*, p. 439).

Not the least tragic feature of all these fervent outbursts is that they are based on falsehood and ethnological nonsense. Science does not admit that civilization is the gift of a supreme "Aryan" race nor does it identify the hybrid population of modern Germany with such a race. Much misty and inaccurate thinking would be eliminated if we could achieve precision in our use of the term "race". To an ethnologist, it can mean nothing other than the

possession of certain specific physical characteristics. The
various breeds of cows are not based on the qualities of
their mooing nor on common association on the same farm.
In like manner, a human race is not a matter of language,
for otherwise the ten million English-speaking negroes of
the United States would belong to an "English race";
neither is it a matter of citizenship, for otherwise these
same negroes would be examples of an "American race".
It cannot be too emphatically insisted, therefore, that the
term "race" is meaningless unless it is scrupulously reserved to designate people belonging to a common type
in such matters as stature, skull-shape, colour of eyes,
skin and hair, and texture of hair.

On this basis, ethnologists commonly classify the 500,-
000,000 white persons of Europe into three main "races":
(1) the Nordic race (Herr Hitler's "Aryans"), relatively
tall, long-skulled, blue-eyed, and fair-haired; (2) the
Mediterranean race, shorter and slighter, with long skulls,
dark hair and eyes, and a swarthy complexion; and (3) the
Alpine race, of stocky, medium build, broad skull, hazel
eyes, and brown hair. The Nordic race, which is a
"bleached" northern variant of the Mediterranean race,
predominates in the Scandinavian countries, northwestern
Germany, Holland, and Britain. It reaches its maximum
blondness in Norway, and its maximum height in the
western Lowlands of Scotland (e.g. Ayrshire), where the
average stature is the highest in all the world. The Mediterranean race is found in its purest form in southern Italy
and in the Iberian peninsula. The Alpine race, as its name
implies, predominates throughout the hill and mountain
regions of Europe, from the *massif* of Central France to
the Carpathians, and then beyond, to east and north, in
Poland and the U.S.S.R.

No national state or linguistic group in Europe is racially homogeneous. The nearest approach to that condition is in the Scandinavian countries, which are predominantly Nordic. In the British Isles, the population is chiefly a mixture of Nordic and Mediterranean, the latter being found mostly in Wales, Ireland, and the "black breed" of the Western Highlands of Scotland. France possesses all three elements, being predominantly Nordic in the north, Alpine in the centre, and Mediterranean in the extreme south. Northern Italy, with its blend of Nordic blondness with Alpine broadheadedness, is in striking contrast to the southern part of the peninsula. The Germans are chiefly a blend of Nordic and Alpine, with the latter element predominantly in evidence. This is more understandable when we remember that historically the Germans of 1,000 years ago were limited to the western half, or even less, of the Reich, and that its extension has been more the spread of its language and rule than any large scale replacement of population. Most of the Slavic-speaking groups are predominantly Alpine in type, although there is an extensive long-skulled substratum underlying what seems to be a more recent spread of broad-skulled Alpines from the Carpathian region, and there is also, among the Russians and Ukrainians, a heavy inter-mixture of Tartar and Mongol elements, due to the long period during which these Asiatic peoples ruled the Ukrainian domain. The Germans of Austria and the Magyars are mostly a mixture of Nordic and Alpine, with the latter element predominating. The Magyars who first set up the Hungarian state in 896 A.D. were a mixed Asiatic race from east of the Urals, but in physical type today they are overwhelmingly European. The vital thing to remember is that there is no "Anglo-Saxon race", no

"French race", no "Italian race", and no "German race",
but only national states bearing these several adjectives.

Community of language, the instrument whereby men
are able to share their thoughts and emotions, is a much
more prevalent element in nationality. There is a very
primitive impulse of indignation when groups of alien
speech settle in a community of comparatively homogeneous speech; and in predominantly bilingual countries,
such as Belgium and Canada, the main line of division and
friction is a linguistic one.

Most of the languages of Europe belong to one great
family, known variously as Indo-Germanic, Indo-Euro-
pean, and Aryan. Certain branches of that family that
spread to Asia include Armenian, Persian, and the verna-
culars of India that stem back to Sanskrit. In Europe, the
family may be divided into six groups: (1) Greek; (2)
Albanian; (3) Balto-Slavonic, including Lettish, Lithuanian, Great Russian, White Russian, Ukrainian, Polish,
Sorb, Wend, Czech, Slovak, Slovene, Croat, Serb, and
Bulgarian; (4) Italic, including Latin and its vernacular
derivatives, Italian, Sicilian, French, Walloon, Provençal,
Catalan, Gallegan, Spanish, Portuguese, Romansch, and
Rumanian; (5) Celtic, including Irish Gaelic, Scotch
Gaelic, Welsh, and Breton; and (6) Germanic, including
Norwegian, Swedish, Danish, Icelandic, English, Flemish,
Dutch, Frisian, Low German, and High German. All of
these languages have certain elements in common; all are
inflected on the same principle; and all stem back in
remote prehistoric times to a common prehistoric ancestor.
Less than five per cent. of the people of Europe speak such
non-Indo-European languages as Basque, Magyar, Turkish, Estonian, Finnish, and Lappish; and as has already
been indicated above, the use of such a language today

proves nothing conclusive as to race. A hybrid language not already mentioned is Yiddish (literally "Jewish", German *Juedisch*), which is a form of German heavily adulterated with Hebrew vocabulary and usually written in the Hebrew alphabet.

It might be well, in passing, to clarify the sense of the term "Aryan", originally a Sanskrit term for those higher castes in India who had imposed their caste system and language on the region about 2000 B.C., but later transferred by some philologists to the great Indo-Germanic family of languages of which these Sanskrit-speaking conquerors were the most easterly branch. The later 19th century saw speculation as to the possible racial unity of all who had originally spoken these languages, and they were pictured as a supremely gifted blond race, that migrated into India, Persia, Greece, Italy, Spain, France, Britain, etc., and then, after creating in each region a great civilization, tended to disappear through being cross-bred with, and outbred by, inferior races. The current use of this term in Germany carries this daring assumption one stage further, and regards the German nation as being, in these decadent times, the chief embodiment of this Great Race. A corollary is their sacred duty to avoid the fate endured by earlier Aryan peoples through miscegenation with "lesser breeds". The chief racial menace is regarded as coming from the 500,000 Jews in Germany. Hence the term "Aryan" in present-day German usage tends to mean "a German whose ancestry is free from the taint of Jewish blood".

What is claimed is that in present day Germany there exists the largest, most important, least adulterated, and most dynamic nucleus of Nordic stock in the world, and that it is a nucleus with its destiny still to achieve. The

Greeks, Romans, Franks, and Anglo-Saxons have had their day, and have either perished or are passing into eclipse. The German glory is yet to come. And if, by an open-eyed preservation of their heritage of race they can avoid the contamination that has ruined their predecessors, there is, they believe, no reason why their civilization should not flower at its height for an indefinite future. Incidentally, this attitude develops an appalling contempt for such nationalities as the Czechs and the Poles, who are regarded as sub-human and hence devoid of any human rights.

The great trouble with these exalted conceptions of an "Aryan" destiny, is simply that they are untrue. The supreme early inventions on which civilization has been based—agriculture, masonry, most handicrafts, writing, painting, and sculpture—were the achievement of swarthy races in Egypt, Mesopotamia, and India at a time when the blond Nordic (*alias* Aryan) was still bleaching in primitive communities in the forests of the Baltic region. The Hellenes were apparently blond invaders from the north, but the supreme achievements of Greece came from the much miscegenated populations of cities like Athens, while a state like Sparta, which tried to keep its "Aryan" stock pure, remained, for all its primitive bravery in war, relatively ungifted. Of the three greatest names in Athenian philosophy—Socrates, Plato, and Aristotle—the first seems to have been an Alpine type, the second a Nordic, and the third a Mediterranean. It is being recognized increasingly that the ancient Roman stock of the great period was very mixed, with a pronounced broad-headed element. As for Germany itself, the majority of its greatest sons—men like Goethe, Beethoven, and Kant—have not been of the pure Nordic (Aryan) type at all, but rather of the broad-headed type which is predominant among the Slavic-speaking nations.

The line of cleavage between groups today is linguistic and not racial, and the false façade of "race" tends to cloak a reality whose organizing force is a national language. Inevitably associated with language are the various aspects of group civilization inherent in human speech— literature in the national speech organizing the whole significance of human life in terms of the mother tongue, not to mention the folk-song and all more formal types of song, all with their roots of emotional association inextricably fixed in national music. Thus it is that about language there crystallizes most fully that form of group consciousness which the Germans call *Volkstum*, devoted awareness of a common tradition and a common culture, embodied in a common language. There is thus a sense in which men of Anglo-Saxon extraction, whether in Britain, the Dominions, or the United States, are conscious of a common *Volkstum*, which does not necessarily coincide with their citizenship, or *Staatsangehoerigkeit*. This form of cultural nationalism is being assiduously cultivated by the present German government; and a special bureau, *das deutsche Ausland-Institut*, at Stuttgart, seeks out carefully all persons of German extraction in every country of the world and endeavours to kindle their proud allegiance to the German cultural tradition. The unprecedented forces of modern propaganda are thus focussed on the task of arousing and maintaining in every state where there are Germans even of the seventh and eighth generation this sense of German nationality of a cultural sort. Of such activities, such composite states as the United States and Canada cannot afford to be unaware. There is a sense in which a proud knowledge of the cultural tradition of his forebears can actually enhance the value of a citizen, provided it does not inspire him with intolerance towards any other national group in the country or make him less ready to fulfil his duties to the state of his adoption. The danger becomes intensified when the national policies of his fatherland and those of his adopted country are sharply antagonistic. Recent investigations of the Deutsche Bund in the United States appear to show that this danger is more than a theoretical one. There seems in many cases to be a definite attempt to mobilize *Volksdeutsche* (Germans in cultural loyalty) into potential *Reichsdeutsche* (Germans owing political allegiance to the German state). There are frequent declarations in the Canadian-German press and from German consular representatives that there is no such disposition to tamper with the political loyalty of German-Canadians. This assertion may, in the main, be honest; but the intensive cultivation of cultural self-consciousness, reinforced by an anti-Semitic bias, may kindle fires that are hard to put out.

In the foregoing paragraphs, we have dismissed race, in its strict sense, as an effective interpretation of modern nationalism. We have, on the contrary, concluded that a synthesis of cultural and historical traditions, grouped about a common language, is the real basis on which a modern community rests its claims to nationality and statehood. Naturally, the larger, the more highly evolved and organized, and the more politically self-conscious a group is, the more likely it is to acquire statehood. The Germans and the Basques provide an instructive contrast in this respect. The former, from Arminius to Hitler, claim nineteen centuries of civilization and 100,000,000 *Volksdeutsche*, some 80,000,000 of whom live in a compact and highly organized state in the heart of Europe. The latter, no less clearly a linguistic group, are few in number, lacking in literature and historic achievement, and live without political group-consciousness, half in Spain and half in France.

Nationality is raised to its most fantastic level of conception by a National Socialist philosopher like Rosenberg, not without debt to the philosophy of Hegel. A brief summary will be illuminating. God is not a personal transcendental Being, but rather an immanent spiritual Force that finds its highest manifestation in the nations of mankind—above all (as history's climax, revealed in our time) in the group-soul of the German nation-state. The individual in such a state is insignificant and his will is capricious, except insofar as he subordinates his whole personality to that divinely inspired phenomenon, the German nation-state. To oppose one's judgment and will to the state's judgment and will is thus not only irrational and unpatriotic; it is also blasphemous, for it is to set oneself against God, whose supreme manifestation is the German nation. On such mystical premises as these, it is understandable that Germans of independent personality find their way to the concentration camp, as the heretics of an earlier age found their way to the stake. On such mystical premises, likewise, it is understandable that Hitler can regard every obstacle to the expansion of Germany's sphere of power as being a sort of sin against the Holy Ghost.

Such theories of national sanctity and national destiny may seem half-insane to citizens of democratic countries. The Nazis would, in truth, be far less powerful were they not supported by habits of thought (the product of historical experience) that set small value on individual liberty or international altruism. The historic German

domain has no easily defensible boundaries of mountain or
sea. From the days of the early inroads of Huns, Slavs,
and Magyars, it was exposed to continual tides of warfare, and national life had to be regimented in order to
make it secure. Government was therefore formulated in
terms of autocratic power, and foreign policy in terms of
national necessity. Under such circumstances, in the long
evolution of Central Europe, the individual has always
been subordinated, first to the dynastic state and more
recently to the nation-state. It was in the relative isolation
and peace of England, on the other hand, that parliamentary government took form; it was in pacific Holland that
religious toleration was first conceived; individual liberty
had a chance to grow in the mountain retreats of Switzerland; and it was in the days of France's unchallenged
hegemony that revolution proclaimed the inalienable
rights of man. We of North America, of a generation that
has absorbed democratic concepts almost without effort,
need to remind ourselves that the political education of
Central Europe has been the bitter legacy of fifteen centuries of warfare, and that the precepts of that education
differ fundamentally from our own. This has been particularly necessary in the years since the War, years during
which we have edified our souls with the comforting belief
that a world system of international law, evolved by a
natural step from our own democratic systems, was about
to be accepted by all the nations of the earth. In those
days, we often failed to sense the unlikelihood of that
acceptance on the part of a great nation, writhing under a
sense of defeat, humiliation, and injustice, and disposed,
both by its political education and by the territorial gains
of the Allies, to regard the whole Geneva system as a
hypocritical subterfuge on the part of successful robbers

who were keeping their loot and proclaiming it an unholy crime for the rightful owner to challenge their title.

Blended with this bitterness has gone a sort of pagan idealism, a reversion, as it were, to the raw heroism of the epic age, which in parts of Germany was never altogether overlaid by the milder attributes of Christianity. For millions of Germans, the philosophy of *Mein Kampf* is a summons to courage, effort, self-sacrifice, hard living, and duty, to walk a stony road through a night-enshrouded wilderness, to regard the individual as but a grasshopper compared to the august destiny of the Nation in a universe of struggle. Here on the North American continent, unlimited individualism and the hedonism of a "high standard of living" have often resulted in a slackness of moral fibre. Many people question why anyone should be ready to die for the principle of nationality (or indeed for any political, racial, or religious principle), when the individual would be equally "well off" regardless of his freedom to practise such a principle. To pass from this to the Nazi national faith is to pass from enervating lowlands into the high, bleak air of an idealism which, though partially mad, is a supreme challenge to courageous living. Contrariwise, it is tragic to find, as the darker side of this valiant pagan idealism, the stain of brutality, ignorance, intolerance, and contempt for such qualities as mercy, forgiveness, love of beauty, or a love of knowledge for its own sake.

A fantastic racial myth has thus issued in a sort of new religion, inspired by the pagan vices and pagan virtues that are still latent even in European man. Another comparison of Hitler and his régime would be with Satan and his defiant commonwealth in the Pandaemonium of Milton's *Paradise Lost*. The griefs of defeated Germany, real or assumed, have been brooded on with "obdurate pride

and steadfast hate"; and infernal courage has been shown
in the defiant rearming of the Reich, with all the desperate
zeal of Mammon's "brigads". Hitler, the analogue of the
grim Archangel himself, surrounded by his Nazi Beelze-
bub, Belial, Chemos, and Moloch, has from the outset been
undaunted in his decision: "War, then, war, open or
understood, must be resolved." But his challenge to
civilization, however brave, is inherently evil and seeks the
dethronement of law in favour of force on earth. He would
rather, like Lucifer, reign in a hell from which all values of
human personality had been obliterated by a race-state
(false in its very essence) than surrender something of
German sovereignty in a truly democratic international
world of civilized men. Germany, under such leadership,
is thus a threat to the entire world.

CHAPTER III

LEBENSRAUM

B ASED firmly on the false dogma of racial lordship and the aggressive impulses of an atavistic tribalism, there has emerged the Nazis' demand for *Lebensraum*, or living space, for the Third Reich. This is the fundamental thesis of their claim against the world today, the standard under which their legions have marched southeast and east. It takes for granted a world of carnivorous sovereign states, each a law to itself, and each seeking to feed its own jungle litter regardless of cost or principle. The national beasts are alleged to differ from one another in value and glory, and therefore the lordliest and most valuable of them all is justified in preying on the rest for the well-being of his own noble whelps.

This is the most naked and unmitigated expression of that rising tide of linguistic nationalism which has become more and more a dynamic world force during the past hundred years. It might be defined as the militant conviction on the part of millions of human beings that all persons speaking a common language are entitled to self-government, preferably in a state of their own, and on the other hand that all areas speaking a common language ought to be united in a common state. As has already been pointed out, this is not a question of race, for all linguistic groups today are hopelessly mixed in ancestry and physical type. Neither does it have any regard for economic law and the simple geographical fact that the principle of a separate state for each language, scattered as all are on the map today, would paralyze world economics and set civilization back for centuries. It is, moreover, a comparatively recent phenomenon, less than a century old, and is only today beginning to affect many groups hitherto unselfconscious. None the less, its disruptive potency has already proved appalling, and no prophet of the world's future dare ignore it.

The nineteenth century saw this principle emerge successfully in the case of the Germans and Italians, but the year 1914 found a Europe in which linguistic and state boundaries were far from coinciding. There were minorities of Celtic-speaking Welsh, Irish, and Highland Scotch in the United Kingdom; Bretons, Basques, and Provençals in France; Catalans, Basques, and Gallegans in Spain; Poles, Danes, and French in Germany; Poles, Czechs, Moravians, Slovenes, and Ukrainians in Austria; Ruthenes, Rumanians, Slovaks, Germans, and Croats in Hungary; and Poles, Lithuanians, Ukrainians, Rumanians, Letts, Estonians, and Finns in Russia. Norway had recently broken away from Sweden; and Iceland was moving towards a further weakening of its union with Denmark. The pressure of minority consciousness was steadily increasing, but it differed greatly in different countries.

It should be remembered, moreover, that the historical past of the various linguistic minorities varied profoundly. Some, such as the Poles, the Highland Scots, the Lithuanians, the Czechs, the Finns, the Provençals, and the Bretons, had enjoyed some measure of autonomous national life within the past four centuries or so, and retained the inspiration of that achievement. The Irish, the Welsh, the Croats, the Catalonians, and the Ukrainians had lost their essential independence at a much more remote epoch, and in most cases had only begun to revive in self-consciousness during the nineteenth century. Still others had never had any independent existence and were people virtually without a history and without a literature in the formal sense. Such were the Estonians, Letts, Ostiaks, Voguls, Votiaks, Lapps, and White Russians of the pre-War Russian Empire, the Slovaks, Ruthenes, and Gypsies of Hungary, the Sorbs and Wends of Germany, the Frisians of Germany and the Netherlands, the Romansch groups of Eastern Switzerland, and the Basques of southwestern France and northwestern Spain.

The almost universal nineteenth century principle that for the sake of national unity only one language should be used in the courts and schools of a state met with different reactions in different countries. In France (as in the United States of America and in the eight predominantly English provinces of Canada), it was imposed without serious challenge. In Germany, on the other hand, while the Sorbs, Wends and Frisians offered no resistance, the Poles (who had been added in the partitions of the eighteenth century) and the Danes of North Slesvig (conquered in 1863) remained obstinately unassimilable. In Austria and Hungary, the Germans and Magyars favoured the principle of uniformity of language in the schools of their respective areas. The Hapsburg emperors, on the other hand, in order to facilitate their control of the many nationalities of their empire, secretly set group against group, Ukrainians against Poles in Eastern Galicia, Czechs against Germans in Bohemia, Slovaks, and Ruthenes and Croatians against the Magyars in Hungary. Linguistic self-consciousness thus aroused, often for the first time, became a dangerous political force; and in Hungary the Magyars in alarm met Hapsburg intrigue with an increasingly rigorous insistence on Magyar as the language of state and education. In the Russian Empire, finally, the Orthodox Church, which dominated educational policy, was ruthless in its insistence on the principle of "one law, one speech, one church", and stopped at no brutality in imposing its programme.

The Great War shattered the boundaries of Central and Eastern Europe, and the Peace Treaties, which set about reconstituting them, paid eloquent tribute to the principle of linguistic self-consciousness. Out of fragments of the former Russian Empire, along the east shore of the Baltic, there were set up an independent Finland, an independent Estonia, an independent Latvia, and an independent Lithuania. Most of the former provinces of Poland, once carved up amongst Prussia, Austria, and Russia, were re-united to form an independent Poland (although 1,500,000 Poles on historic Polish soil remained still in German hands, and Russia still retained historic Polish provinces with 1,000,000 Poles). Denmark, Holland, Belgium, and France received small portions of pre-War Germany. Italy, on the other hand, by extending her frontiers to the Brenner Pass on the north and to the Julian Alps on the northeast, brought 235,000 Austrian Germans and 650,000 Slovenes and Croats within the Italian state. It was in recasting the Austro-Hungarian Empire that the grouping of nationalities was made, if anything, more complicated than before. Jugoslavia, ostensibly a federation of Slovenes and Croats with their linguistic cousins, the Serbs of Serbia and Montenegro, has turned out to be a tyranny in which the Serbs, headed by a dictatorship, have been holding ruthlessly down 4,500,000 Slovenes and Croats, and still other minorities totalling 1,500,000. Rumania, then perhaps the most backward

and corrupt country in Europe, emerged with many
millions of minorities (Ukrainians, Magyars, Germans,
Bulgarians, Serbs, Turks, and Tartars) totalling nearly
one-half of her inflated population. The best of the so-
called Succession States was Czechoslovakia, yet even
here there were elements of positive danger in grouping
together 5,000,000 Czechs, 2,000,000 Moravians, 3,500,000
Germans, 3,000,000 Slovaks, 1,000,000 Magyars, 120,000
Poles, and 500,000 Ruthenes, and pretending that it was a
nation. Considered purely from the point of view of
linguistic nationalism, and its explosive possibilities, the
new order was perhaps even more dangerous than the old,
especially since the groups most discriminated against
were no longer weak and half-selfconscious subnationalities
but the two nationalities of Central Europe with the
highest culture, the most intensely developed national
consciousness, and the clearest historical claims to nationhood, *viz.* the Germans and the Magyars. The Wilsonian
dogma that every linguistic group, no matter how feeble,
obscure, or unevolved, was entitled to national self-determination at the behest of even a handful of spokesmen,
together with the Clemenceau corollary that any such
groups that were friendly to France were to be aggrandized
at the expense of less friendly groups, on military and
economic grounds, led to such a drawing of boundaries as
constituted a permanent threat to the peace of Europe.
Of the two aggrieved nationalities, the Germans, who were
eight times as numerous as the Magyars and had demonstrated in 1914-18 that they were the strongest single
power in Europe, were the force most obviously destined
to challenge the new order when their strength permitted.

The return of the Giant's strength was inevitable, for it
was manifestly impossible to keep the most formidable

nation of the Continent in a state of permanent subjection, and a time-limit of ten or fifteen years might reasonably have been set for that recovery. The treaty-makers of Paris had, it would seem, two clear alternatives: Either to make so generous and reasonable a peace that it would be acceptable to a rehabilitated Germany, or else, having made a punitive peace, to maintain large standing armies to enforce its otherwise indefensible provisions. In the outcome, the treaty-makers made the worst of both worlds. Their peace terms, designed for the military and economic advantage of themselves and the Czechs, Serbs, and Rumanians, constituted a scandal and an outrage to two of the oldest and most civilized nations in Central Europe; but their enforcement was doomed to ultimate disaster when the United States withdrew into confused isolation and Britain as a result refused to ratify the Pact of Mutual Security, and then herself proceeded to disarm on a large scale. The racial dogmas of the National Socialist party in Germany, and the extravagant claims made on their behalf, are in part a measure of the exasperation of Europe's most powerful nationality after twenty years of brooding under a sense of injustice; and the crisis of 1938 was the climax of a long range demonstration of our inability to avert that danger by justice or to repress it by violence.

Associated with the ambition of linguistic groups to attain the fullest political dignity in nationhood, is the even more disturbing economic urge of each such nation to acquire such territorial or other resources as may assure and heighten the standard of life of its nationals. This was the main basis of the successful Czech claim to the German-speaking industrial districts of former Austria, as well as for their unsuccessful demands for the oil regions of

Eastern Galicia and for a "corridor" to the Adriatic. This was the basis of the Slovak seizure of Pozsony (the old coronation city of the Magyars, in which the Slovaks numbered only 12 per cent), rechristened "Bratislava", as a useful port on the Danube. This, too, of course, is the essence of the claim of Chancellor Hitler for *Lebensraum* for the Third Reich, and as such it constitutes the main motivating force with which the present study is concerned. It finds explicit expression in the pages of Adolf Hitler's *Mein Kampf*, but it can best be understood as the naked demand of an intense nationalism for ample access to the means of life and power.

A few quotations from *Mein Kampf* will suffice to indicate the nature of his programme:

Take care that the strength of our nation has its foundations not in colonies but in the soil of the homeland in Europe. Do not consider the Reich safe unless for centuries hence it can give each scion of our race his own piece of ground and soil. Never forget that the holiest right in this world is the right to soil on which one may build for oneself, and the holiest sacrifice is that blood that one sheds for this soil. (*Mein Kampf*, pp. 754-5).

National boundaries have been made by men and altered by men. The fact of the successful acquisition of a vast domain involves no obligation to acknowledge it forever. It signifies at most the strength of the conqueror and the weakness of the conquered. And right therefore lies only in this strength. If today the German nation, penned together within impossible limits, fights against a lamentable future, this is really a command of Fate. . . . The right to acquire land and soil becomes a duty when without an extension of territory a great nation seems doomed to its downfall. This is especially the case when it concerns not some small hypothetical nation, but the Germanic Mother of all life, who has given the world of today its cultural impress. Germany will either be a world-power, or will not exist at all. (*Ibid.*, pp. 740-2, passim).

The future orientation of our foreign policy must be neither to the West nor to the South, but an eastern policy in the sense of gaining the necessary soil for our German people. Since, for this, one needs strength, and France, the mortal enemy of our people, strangles us pitilessly and robs us of power, we must take upon ourselves every sacrifice of which the effects are calculated to contribute to the destruction of French endeavours to hold mastery in Europe. . . . Only when this has been completely understood in Germany, so that the will to live of the German nation no longer decays in merely passive defence but pulls itself together for an active final settlement with France, and throws itself, with the greatest ultimate aims on the German side, into a last decisive struggle—only then will one be able to bring the eternal and in itself so barren contest between us and France to an end; though then only on the assumption that Germany will really see in the annihilation of France merely a means, not an end, so that thereafter our nation will at last attain its possible expansion in another quarter. Today we number 80 millions in Europe. And our foreign policy will be recognized as right only when, in hardly a century, 250 million Germans will live on this continent, not crammed together as factory coolies but as peasants and workmen whose labour will reciprocally vouchsafe life to each other. (*Ibid.*, pp. 757, 766-7).

When we speak today of new land and soil in Europe, we can first of all think only of Russia and the border states subject to it. Here destiny itself seems willing to provide us with a sign-post. . . . Our task, the mission of the National-Socialist Movement, is to bring our own nation to that political insight where it sees the goal of its future fulfilled, not in the intoxicating march of a new Alexander the Great but much more in the diligent toil of the German plough, to which the sword has only to give the soil. (*Ibid.*, pp. 742-3).

Significance is added to these declarations if we pause to recapitulate the resources which the U.S.S.R. has to offer a successful German conqueror. Not least, at the very outset, is a climate in the north temperate zone, adaptable for colonization by white men of the German type. Germany's numerous pre-War attempts to encourage Teutons to settle in the various African colonies of the Reich were an almost complete failure. On European soil, however, within the vastly enhanced Reich of the future, Herr Hitler envisages the possibility of 250,000,000 Germans, enjoying a noble standard of life, and, with that incomparable inheritance of resources, dominating all the earth.

Most familiar of the resources of Russia, especially in the "black earth" region of the Ukraine, is its prodigious capacity for growing wheat and other cereals. In this respect, it is one of the greatest agricultural districts of the world. Less well known, perhaps, is the fact that the U.S.S.R. leads the world in the extent of its timber resources, and that its potential hydro-electric power is equal to that of the United States of America. Most important of all, to a country so industrially competent as Germany, is its almost incredible mineral wealth. At Kursk, for instance, just north of Kharkov, there are forty billion tons of 50 per cent. iron ore, while all the rest of Europe, outside Russia, can only muster up thirteen billions. Even richer in quality is a deposit of over two hundred million tons of 67 per cent. iron ore, now being actively developed at Krivoi Rog, in the Ukraine. In coal, Russia's resources are inferior in quantity only to those of the U.S.A. and China. They total four hundred and twenty-eight billion metric tons, of which seventy billion are in European Russia (nine billion in the Moscow area, one billion in the Urals, and sixty billion of excellent anthracite in the Donetz basin of the Eastern Ukraine). In the allied product, petroleum, Russia easily leads the world, with three billion tons in the Baku region alone. In platinum and manganese, Russia has the world's chief deposits; in asbestos, it is second only to Canada; in copper and potassium it is among the richest of countries. Add to all these silver (in the Altai Mountains and Siberia), gold (Siberia, the Urals, and the Caucasus, with fourth place in the world as a producer), nickel (in the Urals and the Yenisei basin), lead (in the Urals and Siberia), mica (in

Siberia), and chromium (in the Urals), and one has a vision of resources, largely undeveloped, that are beyond the dreams of avarice.

Certain of Herr Hitler's statements suggest that this policy of developing Eastern Europe as part of Germany's natural "living space" is his own brilliant innovation in German policy. As a matter of fact, a careful scrutiny of pre-War policies, especially those of Bismarck and von Buelow, indicate clearly that this had long been the fundamental design of the Reich. Insofar as Bismarck showed any apparent friendship for Russia, it was with the ulterior motive of keeping Britain and France aloof. His major positive aim was to weaken Russia (1) by detaching the various non-Russian nationalities (Finns, Estonians, Letts, Lithuanians, Poles, Ukrainians and Georgians) and making them states under German hegemony, (2) by making Russia itself so dependent on Germany, economically and financially, as to be a great field for German exploitation, and (3) to undermine Russian influence in the Balkans, both as a means to furthering the foregoing designs in Eastern Europe and as a means to building an economic bridge, through Turkey, into Asia. Kaiser Wilhelm II tended to confuse and bedevil this promising programme, for he abandoned Bismarck's sound strategy of taking on only one objective at a time and proceeded, with dreams of an immediate overseas empire as well, to challenge the naval supremacy of Britain. That the major plan of eastward expansion was not forgotten, however, is plainly shown by the treaties of Brest-Litovsk and Bucharest in the spring of 1918. The collapse of the Russian imperial front, together with the inability of the revolutionary régimes to offer any effective resistance, led to the imposition of a peace dictated by Germany. Russia

relinquished all claim to the Baltic and Black Sea regions.
Kars, Ardahan and Batum were handed over to Germany's ally, Turkey. For the rest, there emerged, under
the military domination of Germany, a belt of border
states—Finland, Estonia, Latvia (Livonia), Lithuania,
Poland, the Ukraine, and Georgia. Rumania, although
not a former part of Russia, was reduced to economic
helotage to Germany; while Russia itself, in its mutilated
form, was placed under an economic yoke that was almost
absolute. Had German victory, or even stalemate, been
possible on the Western Front, the Reich already possessed,
in the summer of 1918, the potentialities in Eastern Europe of the greatest industrial empire of all time.

With the defeat of that autumn, the substance was lost
but not the dream. With that dream, moreover, there
alternated the nightmare of encirclement, the boa-
constrictor coils of blockade which had, in the later phases
of the War, taken so heavy a toll of health and life. In
post-War visits to Germany I have found that that nightmare, arising from bitter German experience, constitutes
a definite element in national thinking. Whether it be a
reasonable fear or not, it appeals to one of the most
fundamental of human motives, the desire for survival,
and that is a motive which often puts thought in blinkers
so far as the rights of others are concerned.

A brief survey of post-War movements will indicate that
Germany has not forgotten the East. As early as 1922, the
Treaty of Rapallo was followed by a partial rapproche-
ment between the Germans and the Russians, a rap-
prochement that was sealed in 1924 by the recognition of
a special Soviet Republic of Volga Germans. The Locarno
Pact of 1925 brought its reaction in still closer Russo-
German relations, and the Berlin Treaty of 1926 (extended

in 1931 and again confirmed by Hitler in 1933) provided
for a very extensive participation of German engineers in
Russian industry and for considerable collaboration between the countries, both economic and military. Not the
least important provision was the arrangement for the
manufacture on Russian soil of the military aeroplanes and
chemical supplies which the Treaty of Versailles and the
inspectors of the Allies would not permit in Germany.

The first hindrance to this economic penetration came
from the Five Year Plan that began in 1927. Two years
later, the Bolshevik programme of collectivization drove
off their farms the German colonists of the Soviet Republic
of Volga Germans, and helped to embitter international
relations. The threat of Japanese aggression in the Far
East next led the U.S.S.R. to seek to stabilize its relationships in Europe; and the result was a series of non-
aggression pacts with England (1931), France (1931),
Rumania (1933), and Czechoslovakia (1933). A disturbing
factor was the well known territorial policy of the National
Socialist party, and the embarrassing fact (of which the
Russian secret service became very well aware) that Herr
Hitler was telling the Western Powers that he was ready
to give full guarantees of their security if he was given a
free hand in Eastern Europe. Encouragement to the
Ukrainian nationalists in the U.S.S.R. was likewise ema-
nating from Berlin. The Russians naturally felt themselves
threatened, and countered by joining the League of Nations in 1934 and by signing definite treaties with France
and Czechoslovakia in 1935. The German tactics then
were to organize an anti-Comintern *bloc*, with a view to
isolating Russia.

Out of all this survey, there emerges a very definite
German ambition to conquer, organize, and colonize the

territories of the U.S.S.R. as part of the Herrenvolk's natural destiny and legitimate living space.

For the moment, Hitler seems to have waived this programme by his surprising pact of mutual assistance with Communist Russia. This apparent *volte-face* need not be regarded as a profound mystery. It is most probably the same sort of realistic opportunism that led Bismarck to take on only one adversary at a time—*e.g.* linking up with Austria in 1864 in order to attack Denmark, but with the crushing of Austria still reserved as a future plan. In *Mein Kampf*, Hitler similarly makes clear his opinion that antagonism in Western Europe must first be extinguished by war before he is free to carve out his new German Empire in Russia. The partition of Poland does not help his problem a whit, as Poland was already gravely overpopulated, and the part now acquired brings him none of the essential raw materials on which his dream empire can be built. Neither would his seizure of Hungary and the Balkans, if permitted by Russia, advance his cause greatly, for all of these countries are overpopulated, and Rumania, the richest in resources, will have exhausted all its available petroleum in the near future.[1] Without an ultimate conquest of Russia, Hitler's *Bodenpolitik*, the policy of blood and soil on which he has staked everything, is doomed to utter failure.

So far as reason and justice are concerned, it has been bankrupt from the beginning. It is not merely that the racial theories, which are his major premises, are untenable. The growth and overpopulation which he ascribes to the German nation are likewise false. Instead of being overpopulated, the Reich has actually been compelled to import labourers. Instead of pressing against the frontiers

[1] *Southeastern Europe*, Chatham House, 1939, p. 128.

of Poland, the German rural population of the east was actually shrinking while that of Poland, across the frontier, was much heavier and was increasing rapidly. At the present time, according to official German statistics, the net German reproduction rate is less than unity, *i.e.* is not adequate to maintain the population even at its present figure. Even if the infant mortality were reduced by 40 per cent. and the net reproduction rate increased by 2.3 per cent., the population would only increase slowly from 75,340,000 in 1939 to a peak of 80,535,000 in 1970 and thereafter would decrease steadily to 77,031,000 in the year 2000.[1] When Herr Goebbels prophesies 130,000,000 Reichsdeutsche for 1990 or Herr Hitler 250,000,000 for 2040, their statements are proven by the German Statistical Office itself to be irresponsible falsehoods.

As for Germany's present degree of self-sufficiency in foodstuffs (*viz.*, 83 per cent.) it is one of the highest in Europe. Norway and Switzerland, for example, neither of which has colonies of its own, have self-sufficiency rates of 43 per cent. and 47 per cent. respectively; and although Great Britain, with a scant 25 per cent., has widespread colonies, it must nevertheless pay for the supplies it receives.

Colonies, in the strict sense of the term, are today tropical or subtropical. Their teeming populations combine with climate to make large scale white colonization impossible, and the prodigal increase in commercial output makes abundant supplies of all their products (tea, cocoa, sugar, coffee, fruits, cotton, palm-oil, rubber, tin, copper, petroleum, and phosphates) available at low prices. In nearly all these lines, world supply exceeds world demand. There would not have been the slightest difficulty for the

[1] *Wirtschaft und Statistik*, 1938, pp. 971-5.

Reich to obtain, and pay for, all the raw materials normally needed to supplement its existing supplies, had it not been for Hitler's fantastically large purchases of material for rearmament.

Moreover, a generous share in the colonial and mandated territory of the world would be willingly accorded Germany, were it not for the certainty that its present rulers, whose openly avowed purpose is world conquest, would promptly use these newly acquired regions as aeroplane, submarine, and military bases from which to paralyse and appropriate still further areas of the world.

The slogan of *Lebensraum* thus appears as false and unscrupulous, unsupported either by any expansion of Germany's population or by any fatal lack of food and the raw materials of peace. Yet towards conquered neighbours like Bohemia and Poland, Hitler is inexorable. Concession to him only prepares the way for more inordinate demands, and there is no prospect of any limit to his appetite short of his recorded ambition of world conquest.

CHAPTER IV

THE EASTWARD THRUST: CZECHOSLOVAKIA

BETWEEN the Nazi battering-ram and the Soviet treasure-chamber there stood, two years ago, an intervening wall of nations numbering 112,000,000, in a territory averaging 500 miles in width. It might superficially be assumed that such a belt of buffer states would offer an effective obstacle to a driving-force of only 70,000,000, especially since there lay behind them, in the Promised Land of the Nazi Moses, a well armed nation of 160,000,000, while to the west of Germany stood France and Britain with a combined population of 85,000,000.

The rapid disintegration of Zwischen-Europa ("the Europe in between"), as it has been called, was in large measure the result of inveterate animosities among the smaller nationalities that made up the area. Had they constituted a compact federal state with a unified foreign policy, their hope of survival would have been greatly enhanced. On the contrary, their whole foreign policy was one of division and discord. The three states of the Little Entente, each gorged and bloated with indigestible minorities, had as the primary purpose of their alliance, the perpetual helplessness of Hungary and Austria. Farther north, there was bitter enmity between the Czechs and the Poles, dating from the Czech seizure of Polish Cieszyn in 1919 and the wild scenes of jubilation in Prague in 1920 when it seemed likely that the Soviet army would obliterate Warsaw and the Polish state. The Poles, on their part,

repaid this hostility in kind during the German threat of
1938. A few voices, including that of the Croat martyr,
Stefan Raditch, had been raised in favour of a Danubian
Confederacy, but their appeals fell on deaf ears. Zwischen-
Europa continued a bear-garden of passionate nationalities, even though the Nazi dinosaur, in whose shadow
they lived their little lives, grew hourly in muscle and
appetite.

The share of culpability assignable to France and
Britain for the fate of Czechoslovakia will long be a
matter for debate. In retrospect, the unresisting surrender
of the bastion of Central Europe, leaving the Danubian
lands and the Southeast comparatively open to German
attack, was a calamity of the first order and may yet prove
decisive for evil. The most savage critics of the Munich
Agreement have usually gone on to claim, not only that
the Chamberlain-Daladier capitulation was a disgraceful
betrayal of faith and a fatal surrender of vital military
factors, but that it was at the same time an unnecessary
surrender, since a firm stand would have halted Hitler.
Mysterious assurances from unverifiable sources are
quoted in support of the idea that the Fuehrer was bluffing
and that a categorical negative from Britain and France
would have saved the Czechs.

Even before Munich, out of experience in Europe in
1938, I was a regretful prophet of Mr. Chamberlain's
course on grounds of tragic necessity. The arguments may
be summarized thus:

1. Hitler was not bluffing in September, 1938, a conclusion that is borne out by his 1939 defiance of Anglo-
French intervention on behalf of Poland.

2. There was a widespread conviction in Central Europe
last year, even in many Czech circles, that Russia had no

intention of coming in force to the aid of Czechoslovakia, a conclusion that has been endorsed by the Russo-German pact of 1939.

3. The political life of France was seriously divided at the time.

4. The British and French air forces were hopelessly unprepared for a conflict with Germany. Whatever else may have motivated the Chamberlain policy, it at least gave Britain and France nearly a year's respite in which to arm for a showdown, if that proved inevitable.

5. Granted, as seemed momentarily plausible, a measure of good faith from Hitler, the application of the nationality principle to the discontented minorities in Czechoslovakia was theoretically reasonable enough to make its prevention a bad excuse for a war.

Another unavailing conjecture in retrospect is the different picture there might have been had Poland and Hungary, who were vitally concerned in blocking German expansion, stood shoulder to shoulder with Czechoslovakia in resisting the Nazis. Both countries had very legitimate claims against the Czechs, but in the face of the gathering storm they might well have sunk their differences and presented a united front. So far as Hungary was concerned, however, the country had been so completely disarmed by the Treaty of Trianon that it was in no shape to fight anyone, and even in its search for redress it used petitions rather than threats. As for Poland, it seemed likely, granting, as most Mid-Europeans did, the prospect of an impending Munich Agreement, that the Germans would soon occupy Polish-speaking Teschen (Cieszyn) if the Poles did not; and there had been consistently bad relations with the Czechs for nearly twenty years, due partly to the unremitting policies of assimilation inflicted by the Czechs on the Cieszyn Poles (whom they regarded as being historically Moravians, who needed to be de-polonized) and partly to the use of Czechoslovakia as a base by Communist and Ukrainian revolutionaries.

The sequel in Czechoslovakia is vital to an understanding of the Nazi programme, for it is a tangible object lesson in the technique of the Eastward Drive. Over against the most plausible propaganda in the world one has only to set the seizure and spoliation of Bohemia-Moravia as a complete and unanswerable refutation.

Up to last March, Hitler was able to pose as the champion of the nationality principle in his redrafting of the map of Central Europe. The Germans of Austria and the Sudetenland had been duly incorporated in the Greater Reich, a million Magyars had been happily restored to Hungary, the Poles of the Cieszyn area had been ceded to Poland, some measure of Home Rule had been accorded the Slovaks and the Ruthenes, and the Ukrainian nationalists had been encouraged to look forward to a realization of their dreams. As for the Reich, he had assured Mr. Chamberlain that it desired no alien elements, such as the Czechs, within its borders.

In March, he suddenly revealed that this had been only one of those large, convenient falsehoods recommended in *Mein Kampf*, and embarked on an openly carnivorous programme. Bohemia and Moravia were gulped down overnight. With the loss of the consummately fortified frontiers the previous autumn, the shell was off the lobster and it surrendered to the shark without a struggle. It became evident, as has since been corroborated in the case of Poland, that the Nazi design, true to the original blueprints of the Fuehrer, calls for nothing less than the domination of all Eastern Europe.

What that domination involves has become as palpable as dirt in the case of Bohemia-Moravia. It is not simply the complete confiscation of the Czech military machine, along with its munition works at Pilsen and with accumulated munitions valued at a billion dollars. It is not even the equally inevitable paralysing of all political freedom by injecting German officials into the blood-stream of the state at strategic points. It is rather the unanticipated looting of Czech industry and finance by the Nazi party, as distinct from the German imperial government and even in apparent opposition to the national interest. The racketeering technique began as early as October 1938, through Nazi negotiations with Czech industrialists, whereby, as a price for the protection of their investments in the ceded Sudeten districts, a controlling interest in the Prague Discount Bank was transferred to the Dresden Bank, the latter being under the control of the Nazi party as distinct from the German state. With the sudden seizure of Bohemia-Moravia in March, the Jews, who controlled most of the banks and at least half of the foreign trade, sought to leave the country, but were told that they must assign to the Prague Discount Bank full authority over all their property. (And then Pharaoh hardened his heart, and would not let the Children of Israel go!) Similar mastery, through various devices of economic torture, is being progressively acquired over non-Jewish Czech enterprises, and the profits of all these firms, both Jewish and Gentile, flow through the Prague Discount Bank and the Dresden Bank into the pockets of the high command of the Nazi Party. They have further debauched the Czech economy by setting up a false exchange rate between the Czech crown and the reichsmark and by dishonestly using for purchases nearly three billion Czech crowns in paper currency which they took up in the Sudetenland last autumn and then, having received on demand an equivalent amount in Czech gold, neither surrendered nor destroyed.

The extension of the German *Lebensraum* over non-German areas thus appears, not as the extension of German civilization but as the rapacious assault of a Brown vampire, sucking all the economic life-blood of the victim into its maw. Czech employers and workers alike are being transformed into white coolies, the profits of whose sweated labour go to enrich the ruthless and unscrupulous masters of the Third Reich.

SLOVAKIA

The new German protectorate of Slovakia provides an interesting case-history in the power of nationalism in Central Europe. When the treaty-makers of Paris linked Czechs and Slovaks together in a common state, it was assumed that the arrangement would prove an ideal one; yet a visit to Mittel-Europa in 1938 found the Slovaks one of the most discontented of the republic's minorities. This is only intelligible if we realize the diverging past histories of the Czechs and the Slovaks, and the unfulfilled conditions under which the latter entered the Czech-dominated state in 1919.

It cannot be too strongly emphasized that the Slovaks are not Czechs, and that there is no such creature as a "Czechoslovak". While they speak closely related Slavic languages, Slovak is not a mere dialect of Czech. The differences are about as great as those between the similarly related languages, Dutch and German. I have on my shelves Miroslav Kalal's Slovak-Czech dictionary (published 1924), in which there are 35,000 Slovak words that were apparently unintelligible to a Czech and hence required definition. As a matter of fact, many Slovak philologists find the closest relative of their language in the speech of the Slovenes, lying to the southwest of Hungary.

The Slovaks have never been an independent nation. Back in the ninth century A.D., they are alleged to have been part of the primitive kingdom of Greater Moravia; but from that time until 1918 they lived peaceably in the kingdom of Hungary, with the exception of a brief period in the thirteenth century, when it was captured by the King of Bohemia. So far as the Czechs were concerned, the creation of Czechoslovakia was the restoration of that historic Bohemia which had passed under German rulers in 1306 and was merged in the Hapsburg domain in 1620. For the Slovaks, it was a complete innovation.

There were two documents, on the strength of which the Slovaks were included in the new state. The first was a resolution supporting union, drawn up by a private group of 106 men, meeting in the little Slovak town of Turciansky sv. Martin. The other was the so-called Pittsburg Declaration, signed by Czech and Slovak immigrants at Pittsburg, U.S.A., in support of a federal union of the Czechs and Slovaks. In the Slovak provinces, no plebiscite was ever taken; and a Slovak delegation to Paris, seeking to state the other side of the Slovak case, was arrested by the French police, on the instigation of Benesh, and deported. Monsieur André Tardieu, in his book *La Paix*, explains laconically: "We had to choose between a plebiscite and the creation of Czechoslovakia."

A bill of indictment, recently drawn up against the Czechs by the Slovak "Revision League", contains the following main charges:

1. The Czechs had treated the Slovaks as an inferior people, to be absorbed and assimilated as soon as possible. The promised autonomy under a federal system had been completely blocked. On the contrary, there was rigid centralization in Prague. Even the national identity of the Slovaks was obliterated, since the census lumped Czechs, Moravians, and Slovaks into a single category of "Czechoslovaks", in order to give the false impression that the ruling nationality constituted a majority of the country's population. Through all the Slovak areas, Czechs were imported to take all the higher offices and most of the lower offices in the administration, the law courts, the police force, the post office, and the railways. The number of Czech "carpet-baggers" in Slovakia was estimated at 260,000.

2. Thousands of Czech school-teachers were brought into Slovakia, and undertook to exterminate the Slovak language. The Czech system of orthography was made compulsory and thousands of Czech words were imposed, in order to support the theory of a single standard language (*viz.* Czech) for the integrated "Czechoslovak" nationality. A Slovak university had been promised at Bratislava, but it was named after a Czech, and all its chairs but one were filled with Czech professors. Czech was the language of instruction, and the students were told that their ancestral Slovak was only a bastard vernacular.

3. The Czechs had deliberately ruined Slovakia industrially. Whereas the Magyars, under the old régime, has annually spent large sums in building up factories in Slovak areas, the Czechs undid all this, for the benefit of their own industries in Bohemia. Altogether, 200 industrial plants in Slovakia had been closed by the Czech government and their excellent modern machinery carried away

to Bohemia for use in Czech factories. An example of this process was the iron foundry at Korompa, which had formerly employed 10,000 Slovak labourers. The Slovaks were further forbidden to raft their lumber down stream to its old market in Hungary or to obtain seasonal employment on Hungarian farms. Figures were also advanced to show that taxes and interest rates were higher in Slovakia than in Bohemia.

4. As a result both of the heavy influx of Czech "carpet-baggers" and of the repressive economic policies imposed on Slovakia, a quarter of a million Slovaks were forced to emigrate in order to survive. The great majority of all persons migrating from Czechoslovakia during the period 1922-30 were Slovaks and Ruthenes, the proportion sometimes rising as high as 75 per cent.

5. The Czech police ruthlessly suppressed any attempt at Slovak freedom of speech. The number of instances in which Slovak newspapers were confiscated ranged from five to six thousand per annum.

6. The fact that a million Czech Catholics turned atheist during the War and that the Czechoslovak Communist Party polled nearly a million votes in each national election was a final ground for grievance on the part of a people so conservative and so devoutly Catholic as the Slovaks. On this basis, perhaps unjustly, they felt that the Czech alliance with the U.S.S.R. had ideological implications that were a menace to the religious life of Slovakia.

Much of this is one-sided and grossly exaggerated. One very relevant retort is that the Slovak economy is too poor and partial to be self-contained, and that the Czechs (like the Magyars before them) actually spent more in the province than it yielded in taxation. At the same time, the extreme Sokol group of Czech nationalists, who dominated the political life of the state, does seem to have attempted a rapid assimilation of the Slovaks as a measure of national self-preservation. The peace treaties had faced the Czechs with the terrific task of creating a nation out of six centrifugal language-groups, among whom they themselves constituted an actual minority; and it is not surprising that they should seek, in the few brief years before the inevitable day of testing, to extend their national centre of gravity by transforming their close cousins, the Slovaks, into Czechs. It was the same desire for national unity and safety, together, no doubt, with the impulse to provide for their own folk, that led the Czechs to keep for themselves a relative monopoly in all districts (German, Czech, Polish, Slovak, Magyar, and Ruthene) of the police, judiciary, post office, and railway appointments.

The creation in March 1939, of a separate Slovak state under German auspices did not come as a surprise to anyone familiar with the feeling existing between the Slovaks and the Czechs, and aware also of the Nazi eagerness to intensify and exploit such a situation for the furtherance of their own programme. A measure of Slovak autonomy had, it is true, been granted by Prague after the Munich settlement, but the ubiquitous presence of an intrenched Czech officialdom in state and school, backed by the Czech army, together with the difficulty of even gradually replacing them with Slovak officials and teachers, made exasperated impatience on the part of the Slovak nationalists inevitable.

The Constitution of their new "Christian National Republic", adopted on July 21, 1939, is, however, as tyrannical and illiberal as the old Czech constitution was free and democratic. Only one party, the extreme Hlinka

group, has electoral standing on the ballot, and the Jews
are treated with Nazi harshness. In gaining nominal independence, they have, moreover, found in Hitler a master
whose little finger is thicker than the loins of Benesh.
Slovakia, although its northern frontier along the Tatras
is as rugged as the Canadian Rockies, nevertheless possesses strategic passes for a flank attack on Poland, and a
German army now occupies the hapless little state. It is
as if an obstinate little gopher, quarreling with his bigger
brother, had invited a wolf to help him.

CARPATHO-RUTHENIA

Eastward again from Slovakia lies the historic Hungarian province of Ruthenia, known journalistically for a
few recent months by the misleading title of "Carpatho-
Ukraine". Its predominant population is 500,000 persons
of mixed Ukrainian speech, mostly descendants of a con-
tingent of 60,000 Ruthenians from beyond the Carpathians. At the invitation of King Louis the Great of
Hungary, they settled here in 1378 under their leader,
Prince Fedor Korjatovich, who became a vassal of the
Hungarian crown. The region has been continuously under
Hungarian authority since the first Magyar invasion of
896 A.D. Minority self-consciousness was unknown down
to the later nineteenth century; and the group sentiment
which then developed was not Ukrainian nationalism but
Russian nationalism.

As the post-war history of this area is summarized in
Chapter VII it will be touched on but briefly here. When
the first Hungarian republic, under Count Károlyi, succeeded the monarchy at the close of the War, the Ruthenes,
like the other national minorities in Hungary, were granted
local autonomy under the Hungarian state. This might

have supplied a permanent working arrangement, had not a predominantly Jewish group in Károlyi's cabinet sold out to the Communists and ushered in the Red Terror of Béla Kún. This new government, which sought to set up Soviet machinery in all parts of the state, stampeded the minorities into dismay. In far off America, the Carpatho-Russian Union, consisting of nearly half a million emigrants from Carpatho-Ruthenia, with headquarters at Homestead, Pennsylvania, took a ballot of all such emigrants in favour of their fatherland joining, on a basis of federal autonomy, the Czechoslovak republic that was then in the process of formation. The vote was overwhelmingly favourable, and was used by the Peace Conference to justify the inclusion of Ruthenia in the Czech state. In Ruthenia itself, no plebiscite was ever taken.

As with Slovakia, no effective measure of self-government was granted until after Munich, and imported Czech officials and teachers monopolized nearly all salaried posts. In the few that were not so occupied, considerable favour was shown to Ukrainian émigrés, who came in over the mountains after the break-up of the Ukrainian republican movement and were strongly nationalist in their sympathies. In such matters as education and sanitation, the Czechs deserve great credit for their achievements in this backward area up in the mountains, but on the economic side disaster resulted from the change, for Carpatho-Ruthenia lies entirely on the southern watershed of the rugged Carpathian Mountains and all of its streams flow into the River Tisza, in Hungary. Nature had cut off the region on every side except the Hungarian, whither the Ruthenes had always looked for a market for their lumber and their seasonal labour. This access was now cut off,

and conditions approaching famine became a common-
place in Carpatho-Ruthenia.

In the autumn of 1938, Prague finally granted local
autonomy to the Ruthenes, and the latter proceeded to
elect their own provincial administration, headed by one
Andrew Brody. When this new government, however,
promptly proposed to hold a plebiscite, as to whether the
Ruthenes should be associated with the Czechs or with
the Magyars, the Czechs in a panic, having arrested Brody
on a charge of high treason, appointed by long distance
telephone a Ukrainophile administration headed by Monsignor August Volosin (hence known popularly as "the
telephone premier") and announced that the region was
to be known henceforth as the "Carpatho-Ukraine". Three
months later, after dissolving all parties except the small
Ukrainian nationalist group, they held a successful election, fascist style, with a ballot chosen only from that one
party.

This episode aroused almost incredible enthusiasm
among Ukrainian nationalists in North America, and a
constant stream of expensive cables from Monsignor Volosin kept their press in an uproar. It was assumed that
"Carpatho-Ukraine" had been established as part of the
Grand Design of Adolf Hitler, and that further steps were
imminent, in which the Germanic legions, pouring by
superb military highways through this liberated nucleus
of a Ukrainian state, would proceed to unite all Ukrainian-
speaking regions, redeemed from Poland, Rumania, and
Soviet Russia, into one great state, dominated for the time
being by Germany but destined ultimately to enjoy un-
trammelled nationhood. It was a pathetically beautiful
dream on the part of Europe's chief frustrated nationality;
and it was not least pathetic because it was based on a

delusion. None of all these North American Ukrainians who hailed the "Carpatho-Ukraine" as a first blessed instalment of their national millenium came from the district in question or were competent to speak on behalf of its population. Those who *were* so competent were the same Carpatho-Russian Union of North America whose vote, twenty years ago, had assigned Carpatho-Ruthenia to Czechoslovakia; and the verdict of this group was utterly different from that of the excited Ukrainian nationalists. In order to help explode one of the most successfully publicized myths of modern times, I quote below from a memorandum issued last December by these North American spokesmen of the Ruthenes:

MEMORANDUM

The Carpatho-Russian Union of North America, representing about 500,000 souls, and being the supreme political and national Federation of the Subcarpatho-Russians (Ruthenians) in America, wishes to express its deepest appreciation to the Four Powers whose representatives at Munich declared that in the interest of world peace the Central European national situation can be most advantageously settled on the principle of self-determination of the people and by putting the same into practice. . . .

The Czechoslovak Parliament has already changed the name of Podkarpatska Rus to that of Carpathian Ukraina and in accordance therewith ushered in the Ukrainian language, in spite of the fact that *the Subcarpatho-Russians never were and do not wish to be Ukrainians.* On the contrary, always and at every opportunity they most decidedly object to such tendencies attempting to connect them with or to identify them as Ukrainians. The newest Czechoslovak-Volosin type of policy is an attack against the national life of our people. Disregarding the will of our people and applying terror and the most atrocious methods of force, it is trying to falsify historical facts, despises human rights, and ignores the national love which, through God, is in all of us.

Many arguments could be brought to prove that those who deem or claim the Subcarpatho-Russians to be Ukrainians, are in error. If this were not so, it would not be necessary, for instance, for the

Ukrainians in America to have a separate bishopric. At one time, when the Holy See of Rome sent for us and for the Ukrainians a bishop in the person of the Ukrainian Soter Ortynsky, we, American Subcarpatho-Russians, through many long years persistently fought for and finally got our own bishop of our own nationality. The By-Laws of our organizations forbid that Ukrainians be members. Our language is different; our national conception, conscience, tradition, and aims absolutely and most definitely oppose Ukrainism. It is not different on the other side of the Ocean either. Specifically for this reason, we took note of the Prague Parliament's above mentioned law with greatest embitterment, and we have decided to strive to the very end against every such tendency which intends to annihilate or counterfeit our national identity, and to stifle our people in Ukrainism.

The Representatives of the Carpatho-Russian Union of North America, having been notified of the terrible sufferings of their brethren in their native country and taking into consideration economic, geographic, and historic reasons and existing facts, have decided to turn to every important government of the world with the following petition:

By virtue of Divine and Human rights and by the right of self-determination of people, in order to insure the peace of the world and the tranquillity of Central Europe, as well as in the interest of a better future for the Subcarpatho-Russian people, we ask with deepest respect and full faith in justice, that:—

1. The Subcarpatho-Russian people residing in Czechoslovakia in the territory between the Hernad and Poprad Rivers to the River Tisa, be granted the right of self-determination without delay, under the supervision of an international neutral committee, so that the horrible sufferings of this people be ended.

2. The American Carpatho-Russian Union asks that special attention be given to the fact that the European Subcarpatho-Russian leaders have expressed their opinion that *the fate and future* of these people, both nationally and economically, would be assured in a most practical way if attached to Hungary with full autonomy. The American Carpatho-Russian Union supports this opinion to the fullest extent.

3. The American Subcarpatho-Russian Union most decidedly protests against the ancient Subcarpatho-Russian land being surrendered for Ukrainian purposes, which are hostile and alien to our nation, and would eventually destroy our people's national individuality. Our people never was and does not want to be Ukrainian.

4. Fully aware of our just cause, we solemnly declare that *our people's national individuality, language, original culture, rights and life as a nation, as well as its material-economical progress and welfare cannot be assured within the Czechoslovak State,* and we will therefore fight with every possible weapon and with all our strength in order that the Subcarpatho-Russians may be freed from the present tragical situation, and that they be given the opportunity for a better life, assuring their free development and future, to which every man has the God-given right.

December, 1938. (By the Order of the Plenary Session of the Grand Council, held in Homestead, Pa., November 14th, 1938.)

The Carpatho-Russian Union of North America.
JOHN POPP, *Chairman.*
DR. A. M. SMOR, *Secretary.*

Anyone who has carefully digested this official document will be duly critical of the Ukrainian version of "the Hungarian rape of Carpatho-Ukraine". As a matter of fact, the Hungarian government was flooded all last winter with appeals for intervention sent by the Ruthenes themselves and by Magyar minorities in the towns of Ruthenia. The occupation of the country, concurrently with the German seizure of Bohemia, was resisted only by the small Ukrainophile minority, especially a Ukrainian band of franc-tireurs known as the "Sitch", whose organization had been sedulously promoted by German agents. The majority ideals of the Carpatho-Ruthenians have now been satisfied, for they are guaranteed extensive measures of autonomy, and at the same time can be sure that their economic extremity is at an end, in working co-operation with Hungary.

The cases of the Slovaks and the Ruthenes have been set forth in disproportionately great detail because they so well exemplify the clash of pugnacious loyalties against one another and against harsh economic realities. A separate, self-sustaining sovereign state for every European nationality, large and small, seems a bitter impossibility, destined, if striven for, to perpetuate black hatred and bloodshed for ever.

Two possible solutions emerge from the dust and blood of conflict. The grimmer and starker of these is the incorporation of all these smaller nationalities by force into a conquering empire which would be enlightened enough to permit them (as ancient Rome wisely did) the fullest possible cultural autonomy. Nazidom has the conquest in view, but its savage brain has no thought of encouraging the national cultures and economic well-being of its subject peoples. It seeks rather to treat them as white coolies, the exploitation of whom may minister to the fattening and exaltation of the Master Race; and the incessant insurrection of civilized peoples against any such tyranny would inevitably result in its ultimate collapse. The other alternative is some sort of United States of Europe, in which sovereign states, great and small, are prepared to pool their economic, financial, and political resources, while retaining cultural autonomy in the fullest sense. Such a conception may seem fantastic to some; but even the most fervent nationalist may eventually prefer it to the subjugation of his country or to a savage blood-letting once every generation.

CHAPTER V

THE EASTWARD THRUST: POLAND

THE savagely successful *Blitzkrieg* against Poland in September 1939, has been marked by two things: the spectacular triumph of mechanism over heroism and the equally spectacular emergence of Soviet Russia as an active participant in the partition of Polish territory.

With their mechanized land forces favoured by a phenomenally dry season, and with a superiority in their air force that put Polish field operations utterly at their mercy, the Nazi armies swept like a tornado through the country. Hitler himself spent much time with the invading forces, and seems to have been in part responsible for the implacability with which open towns and cities, including the capital, Warsaw, were blasted into ruin. Nazi penetration into eastern Poland led, however, to a tidal wave of Russian troops sweeping westward over the eastern provinces, allegedly by pre-arrangement, and blocking any further German advance towards Rumania or the Ukraine. The result, for the present, has been a predatory division of Poland, by which Germany takes the western three-fifths with a population of about 24,000,000 (21,000,000 of whom are Poles, 2,400,000 Jews, and 600,000 Germans) and Russia the eastern two-fifths with a population of about 12,000,000 (4,500,000 of whom are Poles and the remainder Ukrainians, White Russians, Jews, and Lithuanians).

Poland's moral and historic rights to nationhood, once more thus brutally extinguished, are of ancient and honourable standing. The Polish state enjoyed a continuous existence of over nine centuries, from the ninth century A.D. down to the end of the eighteenth century, and its reappearance in 1918 was a vindication of its enduring national vitality. It was originally larger even than it is today and at one time it stretched to within fifty miles of Berlin. The pristine cradle of the nation is the province of Poznania or Posen (90 per cent. Polish-speaking). The disappearance of Poland through successive partitions amongst Prussia, Austria, and Russia was made possible by the selfish decadence of the Polish gentry and by an unworkable constitution. An outburst of patriotism amongst the common people and the framing of a new Constitution in 1791 came too late to save Polish liberty. In the regions taken over by Prussia, strenuous efforts were made to assimilate the Poles and to permeate their districts with settlements of German colonists, but ruthless pressure seemed only to harden and clarify the national feeling of the Poles. Polish armies, previously plotted for, sprang into existence when Germany and Austria collapsed in 1918. The present frontiers were, for the most part, won by those armies and confirmed by the peace treaties of the Council of Ambassadors. While still leaving parts of historic Poland within Germany (1,500,000 Poles) and the U.S.S.R. (1,000,000 Poles), these frontiers are regarded by the Poles as legitimate and final.

The difficulties faced by the new state in 1920 were appalling. The reunited fragments of historic Poland had for one hundred and fifty years been adapted to the economic systems of three separate empires and had now to be coordinated on an entirely new plan. Most of the country, moreover, had been fought over almost continuously from 1914 to 1920 and left with its railways, roads, bridges, and towns in a state of indescribable ruin. For years, hundreds of thousands of impoverished peasants in the eastern districts lived in mere holes in the ground. The heroic efforts by which (without those reparations by which comparable but smaller devastated districts in Northern France were restored after the War) the Polish government succeeded in rebuilding its ancient house, constitute one of the greatest achievements of modern times. It was almost inevitable, however, that these economic struggles should have taxed the nation to the utmost and have prevented it from developing an air force and mechanized units at all adequate for national defence. The Polish army had available 4,500,000 trained men, and the morale of the private soldier, whether demonstrated at Westerplatte or at Warsaw, was magnificent to the last degree; but against the German equipment, the Polish army was like a naked man with a sword trying to battle a knight in armour who carried a rifle. Their fight was as heroic, and as unavailing, as that of Kosciuszko's scythe-armed peasants against Russian cannon at Maciejowice.

It is fantastic to believe that there are today any great undeveloped spaces in Poland for German colonists. In the midsummer of 1939, with a population of 35,500,000, Poland was more seriously overpopulated in her arable areas than was Germany. Her birth-rate was much higher, and the country was actually contributing immigrants to German agriculture. Poland, in 1936, had almost as many children of elementary school age as Germany had, although her total population was only half that of the Reich. It is indicative of this phenomenal upsurge of young Polish life during two decades of enthusiastic independence, that 70 per cent. of all Poles are under forty years of age.

Apart from sweet gratification to Nazi arrogance and hatred, it is hard to see what Hitler has won by his slaughterous extinction of Polish liberty. There are some industrial gains in Silesia, and the Polish countryside brings him a little closer to agricultural autarky; but the fundamental objectives of his *Bodenpolitik* are still far off. Even the oil wells of Eastern Galicia are in Russian hands, and the Baltic coast is rapidly passing under Russian domination. A permanent settlement of Europe on the basis of present military frontiers would leave Hitler a bankrupt failure, with his life's supreme purpose thwarted and defeated.

DANZIG

The focus of German pressure and intrigue against Poland has been the Baltic port of Danzig. A survey of its chequered history would therefore seem to be a pertinent postscript to a discussion of Germany's conquest of Poland in 1939.

In its earlier stages it was a Polish town, dating back to the days when the Polish Kingdom stretched almost as far west as Berlin. In 1308 it was treacherously captured by the Order of Teutonic Knights, who massacred ten thousand defenceless Christian citizens of the town, an act in keeping with their general treatment of the Poles. The port became increasingly German in character and in 1360 it formally became a member of the Hanseatic League. Beyond paying dues to the Teutonic Order, it was virtually independent, and grew very rich and powerful. After the defeat of the Order by Poland in 1454 and the reunion of Pomorze and Danzig with Poland, the city's rights and privileges were extended and confirmed in a charter granted it by the Polish King. Inasmuch as the port's prosperity (and almost its existence) depended on the Polish trade of the Vistula basin, it remained on faithful terms with its Polish overlords for the next three centuries and a half. At the same time, as a virtual "free city", it guarded its German culture and character with an exclusiveness that even forbade by law any intermarriage with Poles.

By the eighteenth century a decadent nobility and an impossible constitution had reduced Poland to a state of prostration and its territories were torn to pieces by its predatory neighbours—Prussia, Austria, and Russia. In this international cannibalism, Danzig (along with Pomorze and Poznania) was swallowed whole by Prussia. From 1793 to 1918, Danzig was a mere provincial town, shorn by Germany of all its old rights and privileges and ruined commercially by the diversion of its former trade to Hamburg, Bremen, Stettin and Koenigsberg. Its main importance was as a naval base, but its old commercial glories were gone.

Meanwhile, during the century and a half of their political extinction, the Poles had been purged of their old irresponsibility and disciplined by suffering into a nation of amazing vitality and stubbornness. All the attempts of Prussia, Austria, and Russia to suppress and assimilate them merely intensified the zeal of their national spirit. Out of the "breaking of nations" in 1918 they emerged as a nation of twenty-five million, the most intensely patriotic and self-conscious of all Europe's nationalities.

The treaty-makers of 1919-20 sought to guard the vital interests of this restored nation, without undue injustice to others. Poland, to survive, needed "free and assured access to the sea". Here economic necessity backed up their clear historical and ethnographical rights in the case of the old Polish provinces of Poznania and Pomorze ("the Corridor") but the case of Danzig was more complicated. As a thoroughly German city, it could not be handed over to Poland. On the other hand, the impossibility of leaving it as a German port and guaranteeing to Poland (as the Germans proposed) free zones in Danzig, Stettin and Koenigsberg, was clearly shown in July 1920 when a refusal of the Danzig dockers to handle Polish munitions would have led to the destruction of Poland by the Bolshevik army had not an emergency consignment arrived at the eleventh hour overland from Hungary. Danzig and surrounding territory roughly thirty miles square was therefore constituted as "Danzig Free City", with complete local self-government, but with Polish supervision of its foreign relations. The integrity of the Free City was guaranteed by the League of Nations, which appointed a High Commissioner to deal with all differences between the Free City and Poland.

At first, the new arrangement led to striking prosperity for Danzig. By 1928 the traffic had risen to four times its pre-War level, far more than compensating for any loss through ceasing to be a Prussian naval base and garrison town. A serious challenge soon developed, however, from the new Polish port of Gdynia, built a few miles farther west along the coast, at the tip of "the Corridor", and zealously fostered by means of special rates and subsidies. As a result of this, Poland's trade through Danzig dropped from 1,089 million zlote in 1930 to 376 million in 1938; while that through Gdynia rose from 231 million zlote in 1930 to 1,183 million zlote in 1938. Economic extinction stared Danzig in the face; and the demand for a return to the Reich might have seemed designed to accelerate the process by deliberate suicide, for Danzig without the trade of a hinterland would have no reason for existence, and Poland, if affronted, could have diverted virtually all of her trade to Gdynia. Control of the mouth of the Vistula meant next to nothing, for the scant 3 per cent. of Poland's exports (mostly local) that came down the Vistula would have made little difference.

On the Polish side of the argument must be set the intransigent hostility of the Danzigers, who sought to kill Poland in 1920 and who now played Berlin's game towards the same end. Had there been good faith on Danzig's part, Gdynia need never have been built. Had there been good faith on Danzig's part in 1939, there might have been some possibility of Polish compromise, assuring Danzig a more equitable share of Poland's trade. But since 1933, Danzig had been in the control of the Nazis. All other parties were suppressed; the dreaded Gestapo operated unhindered; and the Nuremberg anti-Semitic laws were in full force. When this Nazi administration demanded the return of Danzig to the Reich, it was obvious that this was only the gambit of a far more sinister game. No city voluntarily commits suicide. It was therefore evident, for even the blind to see, that the real intention was to seize the Corridor, scuttle Gdynia, dominate Poland as part of the *Drang nach Osten*, and incidentally reap a rich revenge by claiming a monopoly of Poland's export trade.

CHAPTER VI

THE EASTWARD THRUST: HUNGARY AND THE BALKANS

(i) HUNGARY

SQUARELY in the path of Hitler's advance to the southeast lies the ancient kingdom of Hungary. Its population (10,000,000) is roughly that of Canada, and its present territory (35,740 square miles) is less than one-tenth that of Ontario. Its rural overpopulation is among the worst in Europe, and the national poverty, since Trianon, is pitiful. Should there be any armed German attack, the chances of successful resistance would be infinitesimal. The frontiers lie open to the west and north; no foreign power is pledged to her help; and until a year ago, Hungary had been completely disarmed, without a single tank, a single heavy gun, or a single military aeroplane. Even the infantry that hastily manned the frontiers at the time of the Munich Crisis were largely without uniforms and proper equipment; and today, after a year of feverish rearmament, the Hungarians are still, as a nation, scantily supplied with cast-off and obsolescent guns and planes, purchased at appalling sacrifice from Germany and Italy.

Thus far, the Nazis have limited themselves, as in most countries, to a preliminary attempt at indirect control, *i.e.* the instigation and support of a Nazi party within the country, in order that this party may impose such policies as Germany desires. The nucleus of this group in Hungary is naturally the 500,000 Germans within the Kingdom;

although many of the younger Hungarians, especially of the student type, have also proved susceptible to the appeal of a jingoistic, anti-Semitic, anti-democratic movement. Month by month for the past two years, foreign observers have been expecting parliamentary government in Hungary to be broken and replaced by a Nazi régime; yet still a semi-democratic administration survives. It has been a game of cat and mouse, and it is hard to say whether its continuance is due more to the self-restraint of the cat or to the agility of the mouse. Premier Béla Imrédy and Foreign Minister Kálmán Kánya were sacrificed to German displeasure last year, but their successors, Count Paul Teleki and Count Stephen Csáky, have shown an adroitness in defending Hungarian interests that won their government a victory in the elections of May 1939. Under German pressure, Hungary has also had to join the Anti-Comintern Pact, enter into trade agreements with Germany on terms disastrous to her own painfully nourished industries, and enact anti-Semitic legislation of a repressive character; but Hungarian nationalism, which has been hostile to German aggression for upwards of a thousand years, is apparently determined not to make a final surrender short of actual brutal conquest. That conquest may be impending, now that Poland has been duly subjugated; but even then one might predict that the Magyar, like the Pole, would prove so indigestible that both these Jonahs would ultimately be spewed out again by the Nazi whale.

During the past year, German efforts have been directed toward trying to exploit Hungarian revisionism in the interests of Nazi expansion. Thus even while they were helping to organize Slovak and Ukrainian storm troops to defend Slovakia and Ruthenia against Hungary, they were also helping to stir up Hungarian irregulars to raid the borders. More recently it is against Rumania that the Nazis have sought to direct the Magyars, in an effort to secure the return of Transylvania to Hungary, but the government, realizing that Hungary would be only a cat's-paw in such a game (conveniently disastrous both to Hungary and to Rumania), has held the movement in check. Whether that control by the more prudent and intelligent elements in the country will continue, is slightly in doubt, for the younger Nazified groups are keen on action; but so far wisdom has prevailed.

Hungarians in general have no desire for war. It should not be forgotten that among the Central Powers in 1914 Hungary alone opposed the War (through Count Stephen Tisza, whose refusal was at first absolute and whose final consent was gravely conditional), but was dragged in on the Austro-German side through its connection with the Hapsburg monarchy. The war casualties of the little country were two-thirds those of the whole British Empire; and in the sequel it suffered three revolutions, wholesale looting by a Rumanian army (involving losses estimated at eight billion dollars), and finally, through the generosity of the Allies at Magyar expense, the loss of nearly three-quarters of its territory, which had been historically Hungarian for over a thousand years. After so devastating an experience, the general Magyar desire for peace is natural.

All Magyars, nevertheless, from the Regent down to the humblest peasant, have been ardent revisionists; and the recovery of lost territories has been central in Hungarian foreign policy for the past two decades. In her claims for revision, Hungary has had two programmes, a minimum one on linguistic grounds and a maximum one on historical grounds. The former would seek to acquire all adjacent areas in which there are Magyar-speaking majorities; the latter asks for all the historic Hungarian lands. In the autumn of 1938, they received by the Vienna arbitration award an area, containing a million Magyars and about 200,000 Slovaks, which had by the Treaty of Trianon been handed over to the Czechs on the pretext of providing a strategic frontier. Another example of a good linguistic claim lies in a broad strip of country along the western frontier of Rumania, west of the mountains. Here there are 400,000 Magyars and only 40,000 Rumanians. The region was never part of Transylvania, but belonged, historically and geographically, to the Hungarian Plain. It was, however, cheerfully handed over by the Allies to the Rumanians, in order to save the latter the expense of building a new strategic railway to northwestern Transylvania and Czechoslovakia. In Transylvania proper, the Rumanians constitute 55 per cent. of the population, while the Magyars and Saxons make up the remainder in the ratio of two to one. Regardless of the historical claims of Hungary, it is unthinkable that the Rumanians would willingly concur in a return to Magyar rule, even though raw Rumanian rule has dragged the whole region down to a far lower level of civilization. A suggested solution for Transylvania proper, in view of the fact that much of its history, through its semi-independent status under the Hungarian crown, had developed a distinct Transylvanian tradition, has been for the creation of an autonomous Transylvania in which the three nationalities (Rumanian, Magyar, and Saxon) would have equal rights; but the sympathies between the Transylvanian Rumanians and the Rumanians of the Regat have steadily deepened during the past twenty years and it is inconceivable that either would consent to this solution without military compulsion.

At a time when Nazi expansion threatens to engulf the whole of central and southeastern Europe, the question of further revision of the Trianon Treaty becomes for all Hungarians (except the young Fascist group that vainly thinks it can ride the whirlwind) a matter for profound hesitation. In the presence of the tiger rampant, the lean little fox loses his appetite.

It remains to be added that in no region of Europe has nationalism so bedevilled the economic welfare of mankind. Geographically the Danube basin is a great economic unit and to carve it up into states on the nationality principle is to endanger the very life of the parts. Compulsory unity, Roman style, under the Reich, might represent one drastic sort of solution of the apparent impasse in this quarter of Europe; but the Nazi régime, judged by Bohemia-Moravia, is more likely to loot and exploit its provinces than to foster them, and has shown no disposition to permit in essence that liberty of national culture and tradition by which the Roman state reconciled its subject peoples. The ideal solution for Danubia would rather be a sort of Eastern Switzerland, in which the various nationalities, realizing the unitary compulsion of geography, would create a state in which all had perfect freedom of conscious nationality. Mr. C. A. Macartney, in his magistral volume on *Hungary and Her Successors*, concludes (p. 496) that such a solution may ultimately emerge: "I believe that the forces making for unity will ultimately prove so strong that a way will be found to adjust the relationships between the different nationalities in such a manner that they will find it not merely possible to live together, but impossible to do otherwise. I think that it can fairly be said of Hungary what Palacky said of Austria in 1848: that if she did not exist it would be necessary to invent her."

(ii) JUGOSLAVIA

Jugoslavia is a country of 15,000,000 people, in which 9,000,000 Serbs have until recently been exerting ruthless domination over 3,500,000 Croats, 1,000,000 Slovenes, 600,000 Macedonians, 500,000 Germans, 500,000 Magyars, and 400,000 Albanians. This heterogeneous nation was brought into being by the Peace Treaties, which judged it natural to detach the Slovenes from Austria and the Croats from Hungary and to unite these Slavs with their linguistic cousins the Serbs of Serbia and Montenegro in a "Kingdom of the Serbs, Croats, and Slovenes". All these kindred "Southern (Jugo) Slavs" proved, however, that in spite of their close kinship in language their profound differences in tradition were a grave hindrance to the success of the new state. The Serbs, by long experience, felt that a unitary state was fundamental to survival, and regarded Slovenia and Croatia-Slavonia as newly acquired Serb possessions, to be ruled at their will. The Croats, on the contrary, had a long tradition of federalism. In 1918, they had voluntarily voted themselves into federal union with Serbia and were unspeakably indignant to find that the Serbs promptly marched troops into their provinces and treated them as if they were a conquered people. Religion accentuated the breach between them, for the Croats are Roman Catholics and the Serbs belong to the Orthodox Church. During the past twenty years, the Serbs have consistently ridden rough-shod over Croat demands for consideration, ruthlessly imprisoning and torturing Croat leaders and even, as in the Raditch case, openly murdering them in the parliament at Belgrade. The Croats, on the other hand, have been maddeningly negative, evasive, and snobbish in their insistence on their (really) superior culture.

German political pressure seems at last to have forced the solution of a question that at times threatened the integrity of the Jugoslav state. With the Nazis in possession of Austria and hence on the very frontiers of Jugoslavia, and with the Croats openly declaring that they would prefer autonomy under German protection to a continuance of Serb tyranny, the stage seemed set for another act of intervention by Hitler. In the circumstances, the irreconcilable Slavic cousins sank their differences, a reasonable measure of local autonomy was granted the Croats, and a Union Cabinet was formed at Belgrade with six Croats as members and Dr. Vladko Machek as Vice-Premier. This was a heavy blow to Nazi intrigue, which had hoped to turn Croatian nationalism in its own favour. Moreover, the Jugoslav army sentiment is strongly anti-German, and even the Croats are strongly anti-German and pro-French. Under-cover Nazi moves to dominate the Slovene part of the railway line from Vienna to Trieste have stirred up additional antagonism. In spite of the close trade relationships between Jugoslavia and Germany, the political attitude is therefore definitely negative. Nothing short of bitter military conquest is likely to make Jugoslavia a Nazi vassal state; and in that state, guerrilla warfare would probably require a permanent army of occupation.

A new major factor in the case of Jugoslavia emerged in September 1939 with the sudden assertion of strength by Soviet Russia. Czarist foreign policy always maintained a keen protective interest in the Slavic nations of the Balkans, both because of a kinship in nationality and because of Russia's strategic concern in the Bosporus and Dardanelles. The mere existence of a Russo-German pact today is no indication that Stalin is not profoundly concerned in blocking any German thrust to the east or southeast. The resolute swiftness with which Moscow occupied Eastern Poland and has since launched a diplomatic offensive in the Baltic States shows the alertness of the Soviet Government as to its strategic interests. Since the new partition of Poland, Russia is in a much stronger position to strike back immediately if the Nazis invade the Balkans. It is not merely that their frontiers now march together from East Prussia to the Carpathians. For the first time in history, Russia sits astride the Uzsok and Verecky passes and is in a position to fling mechanized armies across the Hungarian Plain at the flank of any Nazi army that is southeastward-bound.

(iii) RUMANIA

Rumania is the largest of the Balkan countries, with a population of 18,000,000 occupying an area of 114,000 square miles or a little less than that of the British Isles. As the bulk of the nation is agricultural, the country is seriously overpopulated and very poor. The few industries of the country are largely in the hands of Jews and foreign capitalists. Apart from agriculture, its main resources are timber and oil, both of which, at the present rate of exploitation, will be exhausted in a very few years. Bauxite is the only mineral found in significant quantities. Since 1935 there has been considerable industrial expansion, due almost entirely to rearmament and the development of munitions factories.

Politically, Rumania has been one of the most backward and corrupt countries in Europe. Since February 1938, it has been under a totalitarian dictatorship, headed by King Carol. Against this strong and resourceful ruler, Nazi penetration has been singularly unsuccessful. The pro-Nazi "Iron Guard" of M. Codreanu (warmly backed by Hitler) has been ruthlessly suppressed, and Codreanu and several of his followers, arrested for open murder, were "shot while attempting to escape". The Rumanian upper classes, the army, the Orthodox Church, the old-line politicians, and the Jewish bourgeoisie are all anti-German; and even the peasants, quieted by the post-war agrarian reforms, provide no soil for Nazi agitation. After the fall of Czechoslovakia, Germany, by military threats, obtained very favourable trade agreements (including the right to open new oil wells with German personnel), but in case of any general war, Rumania, especially since her guarantee by Britain, will assuredly fight against German absorption.

Here, too, Russia is a factor to be reckoned with. The rich agricultural province of Bessarabia, to which Rumania had strong though debatable claims, was taken over by Rumanian troops from Soviet Russia during the confused conditions of 1919-20, and the U.S.S.R. has never yet acquiesced in the permanence of that seizure. On the other hand, it is obviously contrary to Russian interests to allow the Germans to enter Rumania; and the break-neck speed with which Russian motorized units surged into Southeastern Poland on September 17, 1939, was a symptom of their eagerness to prevent so dangerous a domination. The Russian occupation of the provinces of Lwów, Stanislawów, and Tarnopol, not only kept the Nazis out of the valuable Polish oil districts but cut them off from that contact with the Bukovina frontier by which direct pressure could be put on the Rumanians. The presence of the Soviet army on the Carpathian passes will also discourage any German or Hungarian designs on Transylvania.

(iv) BULGARIA

Little Bulgaria has a population of 6,320,000 (80 per cent. agricultural) crowded into an area (39,800 square miles) about half that of North Dakota, and of this territory only 40 per cent. is arable. Less than 100,000 are employed in industry; and the rural over-population is appalling. Of all the Balkan states, Bulgaria has been the one most fully under German commercial influence. Two-thirds of her exports have been going to Germany, and her finances have been virtually managed by the Reich.

Within the country there are strong parties of the Left and Right, the latter anxious, with German backing, to press their legitimate revisionist claims against Greece, Rumania, and Jugoslavia; but the present government, a dictatorship with Mr. Kjosse-Ivanov as premier, keeps both extreme groups firmly in check and would probably strive hard for neutrality in the case of the war spreading to the Balkans. The poverty of the population is such that the shock of war would probably push them into revolution, with still no hope of individual betterment because of the indigence of the whole country itself.

The gains of Russia at German expense have been recently very marked in the case of Bulgaria. With the sudden assertion of Russian "protective" interests in areas threatened by Hitler, there has come a keenly solicitous attitude towards the little Slavic brother in Sofia; and this political interest is apparently to be implemented by a commercial treaty in which Russia will almost entirely displace Germany as the monopolist customer of Bulgaria.

(v) GREECE

Greece has a population of 7,000,000 in an area of 50,200 square miles (almost exactly the same as that of England), but the surface is so mountainous that less than 16 per cent. is arable. She has no coal or oil, and her minerals are negligible. In spite of all this, her standard of living is the highest in southeastern Europe, a paradox accounted for by her part in foreign trade, for she has one of the largest merchant marines in the world.

Since August 1936, Greece has been under the military dictatorship of General Metaxas, an ardent pro-German. The German hold on Greek economic life is extensive, and Germans enjoy many administrative posts. In these circumstances, the recent British guarantee of Greece against aggression has many intriguing angles. In any case, in view of the vulnerability of her merchant fleet to the British navy or to Italian submarines, Greece would never willingly be anything but a neutral.

(vi) TURKEY

A final mention should be made of Turkey. The Turkey of 1914, which became the ally of Germany, was flabby and decadent; but the New Turkey, organized by Kemal Pasha, and now under the strong hand of President Inönü, is alert, vital, and resolutely determined to be a vassal to no one. The population is only 16,000,000, but its strategic position astride the Straits, and barring further by its mountain ranges in Asia Minor the German drive towards Iraq and Iran, is supremely strong. Definitely aligned today against German aggression and backed by British guarantees, Turkey might well be one of the deciding factors, if, in the course of a long struggle, the German thrust to the southeast reaches the Dardanelles and the Bosporus.

Italy has in recent years constituted a more immediate threat to Turkey than the more distant Germany. Not only from their strong naval bases in the Dodecanese but also from the interior of Albania, opening a path to Salonica, and thence to the Straits, the Italians have since last spring been a cause of great anxiety to the Turks. The Good Friday *coup* in Albania was not necessary to bring Albania under Italian domination, for it was already a puppet-vassal. Italian invasion was rather an open menace to Greece and Turkey, and a warning that in case of a German drive on the Straits, Italy intended to be there first. It is this Italian threat, as much as the German one, that has made the Turks so ready to enter into defensive alliance with Britain.

The necessity of keeping the peace with Soviet Russia is, however, not lost sight of. Turkey, like Canada, lives next door to a giant, and a refusal to contemplate war with that giant is a cardinal principle in the foreign policy of both countries. Inasmuch as Russian interests also require that neither Germany nor Italy should control the Straits, the Anglo-Turkish alliance should not be incompatible with Russian policy, provided always that Stalin can be satisfied that British oil-imperialism has no designs on Baku.

CHAPTER VII

THE UKRAINIAN QUESTION

A S A POSSIBLE lever to pry open the rich resources of the U.S.S.R., Hitler has from time to time shown a disposition to encourage such a Ukrainian nationalist movement as might supply him with a large vassal state for exploitation. The encouragement has not been emphatically and explicitly maintained, because the Nazi policy, while clear as to its ultimate objectives, is highly opportunist as to the tactics of the moment and is prepared to sign alliances in any direction to gain a temporary advantage, only to tear up its pledges a month later as a greater advantage appears elsewhere. A Ukrainian puppet-state would nevertheless provide the greatest colour of justice and legality to any Hitlerian seizure of southern Russia, and there seems little doubt that such a state would be set up if the *Drang nach Osten* should ultimately reach Kiev. Under a strong military and police régime like the U.S.S.R., there is no other possibility of a Ukrainian national movement gathering head; and many Ukrainian patriots, while cynical as to any real sympathy on Hitler's part, have been ready to accept his aid, in the belief that after a generation or less the German control would weaken and Ukrainian liberty would grow progressively more real in the Ukrainian state. There are, however, so many mutually antagonistic schools of Ukrainian policy, and even large groups with no policy at all, that a survey of this problem, affecting by kinship the largest Slavic minority in Canada, is much to be desired.

The Ukrainians are the largest European nationality without an independent state of their own. Their numbers today are variously estimated at from 40,000,000 to 50,-000,000, living for the most part in the Ukrainian Soviet Republic (30,000,000 to 40,000,000) and the remainder in Southeastern Poland, the Rumanian provinces of Bukovina and Bessarabia, and, more sparsely, in the Hungarian province of Ruthenia. The Ukrainians speak a Slavic language almost as closely related to Russian, Polish, and White Russian as broad Lowland Scotch is to standard English. So close is the resemblance that there are no linguistic obstacles to courtship and these groups have therefore intermarried by the million. On the other hand, a growing consciousness of language differences, in part reinforced by religious differences, has during the past century given rise to a nationalistic movement of rapidly increasing momentum.

It is important to remember that Ukrainian nationalism is so recent a phenomenon that in many areas no consciousness of it exists, and the peasants, though Ukrainian-speaking, regard themselves simply as a branch of the Russian nation, variously describing themselves as "Ruthenian" (*i.e.* Russian), "Rusin", "Russnyak", "Little Russian". This is particularly the case in Bessarabia, Carpathian Ruthenia, Volhynia, and the urban populations of the Ukraine. Even in Eastern Galicia, the Polish census of 1930 shows 1,139,000 "Ruthenians", 1,675,000 Ukrainians, 2,926,300 Poles, and 421,000 Jews. Keeping in mind the very recent and partial character of this national consciousness, however, it is nevertheless possible to go back and record the early history of Ukrainian-speaking states (if not of nations in the modern sense). As with the rest of the Russian world, Scandinavian dynasties carved out principalities for themselves in Ukrainian-speaking areas during the ninth and tenth centuries, especially the Duchy of Kiev, which is believed for a time to have united all the South Ruthenian tribes under a single authority. Among the notable rulers of Kiev were Vladimir (A.D. 972-1015), Jaroslav the Wise (1019-1054), and Vladimir Monomakh (1113-1125). The Christian principality of Kiev was overwhelmed by a Tartar conquest in the thirteenth century. Farther west, in modern Galicia, the conquests of Vladimir in the tenth century had been recorded by Nestor, the first chronicler of Ruthenia: "In the year 981 he went against the Poles and occupied their Grody Chervienskie (Galicia) with Przemysl". Following the Tartar invasion and the fall of Kiev, the Poles and Lithuanians progressively occupied the former Ruthenian territories in Galicia, Volhynia, and the Black Sea area; and with the personal union of Poland and Lithuania in 1386 all of the Ukrainian lands passed under their joint rule. There was a brief episode of independence in the southern area under the Cossack "hetman" (German *Hauptmann*, "captain") Bohdan Chmielnicki, who defeated the Poles in 1649, only to have part of his domain pass under the power of Moscow. Another hetman, Mazeppa, sought independence from Russia by joining in 1709 with Charles XII of Sweden against Peter I of Moscow; but their defeat at Poltava crushed the attempt. The partitions of Poland in 1772 and 1795 gave Polish Galicia, as well as Moldavian Bukovina, to Austria, while Poland's Ukrainian provinces of Volhynia, Podolia, Braclav, and Kiev went to the share of Russia. Under Polish rule, the townspeople and upper classes had become almost completely polonized and millions of Polish peasants had also settled amongst the Ukrainian-speaking peasantry.

In the areas under Russia, a ruthless programme of russification ensued, including a prohibition (1876-1905, 1906-
17) of the public use of Ukrainian and of the printing or
importing of books in that language. As a result, most of
those townspeople throughout the Russian Ukraine who
were not Russian Jews tended to be Slavs who spoke
Ukrainian but regarded themselves as Russian. Ukrainian
nationalism had most of its roots among the peasantry,
where such leaders as the poet, Taras Shevchenko, had
their origin. In Austria, on the contrary, the rule of the
Hapsburgs encouraged Ukrainian nationalism as an offset
both to Polish nationalism and to the very widespread
pan-Russian sentiment that led very large Ukrainian
groups to regard themselves as "Ruthenians". As a result
of this policy, the Ukrainians were allowed their own
schools, libraries and museums and were permitted to
print their own newspapers and books. In the little
Carpathian community under Hungary, the Ukrainian
movement was entirely unknown. The only members of
the group with a political complex regarded themselves as
"Russniaks", with Russian as their literary language. The
local dialects, some fourteen in number, were undeveloped
and so saturated with Slovak and Magyar elements as to
show no immediate identity with Ukrainian.

THE UKRAINIAN REVOLUTION

In nineteenth century Russia, Ukrainian nationalism
worked underground and expressed itself chiefly in a small
group of Ukrainian intelligentsia. Its political significance
was first manifested in connection with the first Russian
parliament (Duma) in 1906, when a number of deputies
from South Russia declared themselves to be Ukrainians
and formed their own club (Ukrainska Hromada). In the

second Duma, these deputies, now numbering fifty, demanded autonomy for the Ukraine. In the first years of the World War, any symptoms of a Ukrainian movement were ruthlessly suppressed; but with the outbreak of the Russian Revolution in March 1917, the question became a burning one.

Its ultimately unsuccessful issue was in part due to serious divisions among the people. To begin with, the Ukrainians (80 per cent. of the total population) were overwhelmingly peasant in character; while the majority of persons in the towns were Jews, Russians, and Poles, all of whom were uniformly hostile to Ukrainian nationalism. Even in the country, the majority of the great landowners were Russians or Russified Ukrainians. Most of the Ukrainian Nationalists were predominantly Socialist ("Menshevik"), or at least favoured such a confiscation of the big estates as would appeal to the peasantry. The Russians and Jews and the Ukrainian urban workers tended on the contrary to be thoroughly Communist ("Bolshevik") in allegiance, and to favour a close association with Moscow. The landowners were naturally hostile to both the other groups.

Immediately after the abdication of the Czar in March 1917, the Ukrainian Nationalists organized a Central Ukrainian Council at Kiev. A Ukrainian National Congress, held the following month, elected an Executive Committee, of which Professor Michael Hrushevsky was chairman. Relations with the temporary (Kerensky) government at St. Petersburg grew more and more strained; for the latter refused to countenance demands for (1) Ukrainian autonomy, (2) the separation of the Ukrainian soldiers from the army, and (3) agrarian reform, until such time as an all-Russian parliament was duly held. Meanwhile, the Bolsheviks, as a tactical move, promised the Ukrainians autonomy or even independence, in case they seized power. That seizure came with the Bolshevik Revolution of October 1917 and on November 20 a proclamation was issued, announcing the independence of the Ukraine (the provinces of Kiev, Podolia, Volhynia, Chernikov, Poltava, Kharkov, and Taurida), in federation with the Russian Republic.

At first, the "Ukrainian Republic of the People", as represented by Prof. Hrushevsky's Central Ukrainian Council, was content to sit back and watch the civil war between Government and Bolshevik troops, but in December 1917 its refusal to let Bolshevik troops pass through to crush movements in the Don and Ural districts led to a state of war with Bolshevist Russia. At the same time, the pro-Bolshevik and Russophil elements in the Ukraine, together with many sincere Nationalists who preferred to put their money on the Red horse, organized a rival Ukrainian government at Kharkov, and declared the Kiev government duly dissolved. (Most famous among the members of this Red Ukrainian group has been General Voroshilov, destined, as it proved, to be commander-in-chief of the armies of the U.S.S.R.) There were thus two completely organized administrations in the Ukraine, a Pink one at Kiev and a Red one at Kharkov, both claiming to represent the Ukrainian nation. There was therefore elation in the Pink Kiev government when on February 8, 1918, Germany and Austria-Hungary signed a separate peace treaty at Brest-Litovsk with their delegation, as representing the Ukrainian Republic. This triumph was short-lived, for soon afterwards the Red Kharkov government, backed by superior Bolshevik forces, captured Kiev and dealt with their opponents in the spirit of a Marius or a Sulla.

By the Treaty of Brest-Litovsk, the Germans had been promised vast supplies of urgently required foodstuffs from the Ukraine; but the disastrous defeat of the Pink Nationalist régime thwarted their hopes. German armies therefore moved swiftly in on the Ukraine and were soon in possession of Kiev. In setting up a new administration, they were naturally favourable to conservative rather than to radical elements. The old landowning gentry, both Russian and Russo-Ukrainian, together with the old bureaucracy displaced by the Revolution, rallied to their support, and one of these aristocrats, Paul Skoropadsky, a landowner and a former general in the Russian Imperial Army, was appointed by the Germans as Hetman of the Ukraine. In a proclamation of April 30, 1918, the new White ruler (supported by German bayonets) proclaimed the dissolution of the old Central Council of Hrushevsky, the restoration of private property, and the nullification of all the laws of both the Pink and the Red régimes. It was soon evident that the Hetman planned a complete restoration of the social order of Russian times, with himself as a virtual monarch; and a state of civil war developed between the radicals and peasants on the one side and Skoropadsky and the old propertied class (plus the Germans) on the other. The authority of the Hetman was null except in those centres where there were German garrisons, while elsewhere there was comparative anarchy.

The collapse of Germany in Western Europe spelled the end of the Skoropadsky régime. The remnants of the old Central Council speedily formed a Directorate of the Ukrainian Republic of the People, with Vynnychenko as president and Simon Petlura as commander-in-chief of a rapidly growing army. The Germans were glad to evacuate, taking Skoropadsky with them, disguised in a German uniform. Petlura entered Kiev on the 14th of December, 1918. Since other Ukrainian Nationalist forces were at this time fighting against the Poles for the control of Eastern Galicia (the so-called "Western Ukraine"), there was for a time the hope of uniting all the Ukrainians in a single independent republic. As before, however, the Pinks still had the Reds to reckon with; for the latter, advancing in force, captured Kiev on February 4, 1919, and drove the Directorate headlong westward towards Poland.

There in the West, the capitulation of the Central Powers in November 1918 had been followed at once by Ukrainian action. The immediate object of their attack was the city of Lwów (Lemberg), the centre in East Galicia of both Polish and Ukrainian cultural life, and the coveted capital of their projected Republic of the Western Ukraine. Unfortunately for the Ukrainians, the overwhelming majority of the population were Poles and Jews, and when a Ukrainian army, fully equipped by the Austrians in the interests of an ambitious arch-duke (anxious to play the Skoropadsky rôle) seized the defenceless city in November 1918, they were driven out within forty-eight hours by the civilian population. Men, women, and children of the intensely Polish city joined in a fiercely contested battle from house to house and street to street, and then, barricading the freed city, successfully withstood a siege until a Polish army arrived, six months later, and permanently repulsed the Ukrainians. The tide of battle then rolled farther east, with its outcome predominantly in favour of the Poles. In June 1919, the Ukrainians enjoyed brief success in a local offensive at Czortków, in the extreme southeast, but in the following month they retreated once more, beyond the Zbruch River.

April 1920 saw an amicable agreement between Simon Petlura's Ukrainian government and Joseph Pilsudski's new Polish state, whereby the Ukrainian government received a promise of Polish assistance in liberating Kiev and the whole right bank of the Dnieper, abandoning at the same time all claims to Eastern Galicia and Western Volhynia. The demarcation line of the Polish and Ukrainian states, as approved by this agreement, corresponds roughly to the 1920-39 eastern frontier of Poland. The first stages of the ensuing offensive were favourable to the combined Polish and Ukrainian armies of Pilsudski and Petlura; and on May 8, Kiev changed masters again, for the seventh time in three years. Meantime, however, the Bolshevik armies had defeated the White Army of General Denikin and were able to concentrate very strong forces against the restored Pink state and its Polish backers. The Bolsheviks once more occupied Kiev, and the Polish-Ukrainian army began a stubbornly contested retreat, which did not stop until the decisive Battle of Warsaw, almost within gunshot of the Polish capital, definitely crushed the Bolshevik advance. Poland was now economically exhausted, and needed peace. An armistice with the Russians was therefore signed on October 18, 1920, and was duly followed by the Treaty of Riga on March 18, 1921. By this, the Russo-Polish frontier was drawn as it stood till 1939. So far as the predominantly Ukrainian areas were concerned, Volhynia and Eastern Galicia remained with Poland, while in the area under Russian control a Ukrainian Soviet Republic was duly confirmed, federated with the Union of Socialist Soviet Republics. This was equivalent to the triumph of the Red Ukrainian government that had been organized at Kharkov in 1917. As has been already noted, there were marked national

elements in this group, and many of them regarded this
settlement as the ideal realization of Ukrainian nationhood, especially in view of the Communist proclamation in
Moscow in December 1917 of a "Declaration of the Rights
of the People of Russia", recognizing the equality of rights
of all the nations of Russia, their right to self-determination and to secession, and the right of national minorities
to free development.

SUBSEQUENT DEVELOPMENTS

As early as 1923, there were signs that the independence
of the Ukrainian Soviet Republic had a dubious future;
for in that year, by a pact of federation, the Republic
resigned its sovereignty in favour of the U.S.S.R. in all
matters of foreign affairs, the army, transport, the post
office, foreign trade, industry, and finance. The only
domains left to the Ukrainian Republic were agriculture,
justice, education, and public health. In keeping with this
limited autonomy, the Ukrainian language was freely
introduced into the schools and into public life; but the
result was to cause such an increase in nationalistic tendencies as to incur the grave displeasure of the Russian
central authorities. As early as 1928, sharp friction developed between Moscow and the nationally-minded government at Kiev. In 1933, open conflict broke out, when
Moscow's efforts to collectivize Ukrainian agriculture led
to such resistance that the All-Russian government ac-
cused the Ukrainians of betraying Communism for the
sake of nationalism. Dire repression was applied at once.
Most of the men who had helped to organize the Ukrainian
Soviet Republic were arrested and replaced by new men,
chiefly Russians, who were hostile to Ukrainian ideals,
and the national gains of ten years were wiped out in a few

weeks. The whole Ukrainian world was moved by two despairing suicides, those of Nicholas Hylovy, the most eminent Ukrainian writer of the day, and of Nicholas Skrypnik, former Commissar for Education in the Ukrainian Soviet Republic and a personal friend of Lenin. The Ukrainians intensified their resistance, but the control from Moscow was unyielding, and the result was a famine in which upwards of 5,000,000 Ukrainians died of starvation. Nor have conditions improved much since that time. In August 1937, Panas Lubchenko, a genuine Communist and a genuine Ukrainian, head of the Ukrainian Soviet Republic from 1933 to 1937, added his suicide to the significant list of those who have sought thus to protest on behalf of the Ukraine's extinguished liberty. National feeling is probably higher in the Ukraine today than ever before; but the day of its realization seems to be a long way off.

Under the Polish government, likewise, the Ukrainian issue was still far from a solution. Originally, Eastern Galicia had been assigned to Poland under mandate, subject to reconsideration by the League of Nations after twenty-five years; but in March 1923, Poland was given the whole region unconditionally by the Council of Ambassadors. In these circumstances, the Ukrainians tended to constitute the "Irish Question" of Poland. There was, as in the case of the Irish, a predominant difference in religion, since the Ukrainians and Ruthenians belonged either to the Greek Orthodox Church or to the Uniate Church (a branch of the Catholic Church, with a married clergy and the use of the Eastern ritual), while the Poles were Roman Catholics of the strictest school. The Ukrainians and Ruthenians were in the majority in the rural parts (although even here there were over 2,000,000 Poles, everywhere intermarried with the others), while the Poles had for the past five and a half centuries been the dominant race in the towns and cities. Lwów in particular is a sort of intensely Polish Belfast set down in a Ukrainian Munster and coveted by the Sinn Fein. In spite of its predominantly rural character, the Ukrainian community has shown great cultural vitality, especially in such institutions as the Ridna Shkola Association, the Prosvita Association, the Peter Mohyla Institute, the Taras Shevchenko Scientific Society of Lwów, and the Ukrainian Scientific Society of Warsaw. In the matter of agricultural co-operatives, the Ukrainians have shown distinctly greater capacity than the Poles.

There have been numerous political parties among the Ukrainians of Poland: the Hetman Party, the Classocrats, the Ukrainian National Rebirth Party, the Ukrainian Catholic Alliance, the Ukrainian National Democratic Party, the United National Front, the Volhynian Ukrainian Union, the Ukrainian Peasant Party, the Ukrainian Socialist Radical Party, the Ukrainian Social Democratic Party, the Organization of Ukrainian Nationalists (O.U.N.), the Ukrainian Warring Organization (U.W.O.), and the Communist Party of the Western Ukraine. The majority of these parties have sought, through their representatives in the Polish parliament, to achieve "Home Rule" within the Polish state, as a step towards the ultimate uniting of all Ukrainian territories in an independent Ukrainian state. While not very sympathetic towards this more remote objective, there have been many Polish leaders working constantly for an amicable solution of the Ukrainian Question on a Home Rule basis, and in this they have been met half-way by many prominent Ukrainians. The whole issue has been badly compromised by the

O.U.N. and the U.W.O., two outlawed terrorist organizations, corresponding to the Irish Republican Army. Inspired by the same sort of perverted patriotism, they have repeatedly and ruthlessly assassinated not only important Poles but a host of the Ukrainian leaders, great and small, who have been striving for co-operation with the Poles. Prominent among these victims of political murder have been Thaddeus Holowko, prominent in the Ministry of the Interior; Bronislaw Pieracki, Minister of the Interior; M. Babiy, principal of the Ukrainian Secondary School at Lwów; and W. Sobinski, curator of the School District of Lwów. From July to November 1930, the terrorist organizations began a widespread and carefully planned programme of murder, violence and arson throughout Eastern Galicia, with a view to demoralizing the Polish administration and forcing the intervention of other Powers. The result, however, was a swift and pitiless campaign of "pacification" by a special corps of Polish military police, whose activities were comparable to those of the "Black-and-Tans" in Ireland's dark history. Rifles, revolvers, and bombs were confiscated on a large scale; but the police proceeded likewise to wreck a great number of the Ukrainian co-operatives and community centres, alleging that these were foci of insurrection.[1] A further unhappy episode occurred in the summer of 1938, when over a hundred Orthodox church buildings in Volhynia were either destroyed or transferred to the Roman Catholic Church. The counter-argument is that nearly all of these parishes were forcibly transferred from the Catholic church to the Ortho-

[1]The O.U.N. has its present headquarters in Jugoslavia, with other centres in London, Paris, New York, and Saskatoon. It is still active, and maintains, largely with American and Canadian funds, a Ukrainian Press Bureau in London, a periodical in Paris, and the "Ukrainian Press Service" in New York.

dox church by the Russian government during the nineteenth century; but after a couple of generations the change back probably represented a dislocation of equal violence and one therefore most unfortunate, to say the least. As for the small Ukrainian Communist Party in Poland, it has consistently advocated the union of the Ukrainian and White Ruthenian areas of Poland with the Ukrainian and White Ruthenian Soviet Republics directly to the east; but Moscow's campaign of repression in the Ukraine since 1933 has caused its influence to disintegrate.

Under the police and military régime of Rumania, the Ukrainian movement in Bukovina and Bessarabia has never gained any momentum. The most dramatic episode of recent times has rather been associated with Subcarpathian Ruthenia, a region where Ukrainian consciousness was unknown before 1918 and such few anti-Magyar stirrings as existed were Russian in their orientation. At the close of the War, three main claimants for the territory emerged: (1) a Ruthene council at Ungvár accepted and ratified an autonomous régime, as part of Hungary, proposed by the new Hungarian's People's Republic of Count Károlyi; (2) a Ruthene council at Preshov (now in Slovakia), instigated by invading Czech troops and backed by a Czech-negotiated plebiscite of Ruthenian-American immigrants in the U.S.A., voted in favour of federation with "Czecho-Slovakia" on an autonomous basis; and (3) a third Ruthene council, in Huszt, organized by an invading detachment of Ukrainians from Eastern Galicia, demanded union with the Ukraine. An election held in March 1919 gave a large majority in favour of the first solution; but Béla Kún's brief Communist régime in Hungary supervened, the Rumanian and Czech armies occupied all of Ruthenia, and the second solution (autonomous federation with Czechoslovakia) was duly approved by the treaty-makers at Paris. Under Czechoslovakia, along with much excellent work in justice, public works, public health, and education, there went a confusion of policies as to nationality. A flood of refugee Russian Orthodox priests was turned loose on Ruthenia in the spring of 1921, and not only proselytized vigorously from the pro-Magyar Uniates but greatly strengthened the place of Russian as a language of education. On their heels came an even larger flood of Ukrainian refugees from Eastern Galicia, for whom the Czechs cordially founded two universities, at Prague and Podiebrad, and furnished extensive employment in Ruthenia, especially in administration and in the schools (where they inaugurated a feverish Ukrainophil movement). To counterbalance these two violently antagonistic movements, the Czechs also, more recently, sought to encourage, in elementary education, the local Ruthenian dialects rather than the more alien Russian and Ukrainian literary languages, and took steps to restrain the more zealous propaganda of the Russifiers and the Ukrainizers.

Such was the background in the autumn of 1938, when the dissolution of Czechoslovakia grew imminent. Harking back to the original autonomy proposals of 1919, Ruthenia was given extensive measures of Home Rule. When, however, the duly elected Ruthenian government of Andrew Brody proposed a plebiscite on the issue of reunion with Hungary, it was disbanded by the Czech police and imprisoned for treason; and the minority Ukrainian group, headed by Monsignor Volosin, was appointed by long distance telephone from Prague and supported by Czech troops. It was generally believed that Nazi Germany was prepared to back this Ukrainophil administration as a pass-key to open the Ukrainian regions beyond the Carpathians and inaugurate a great Ukrainian state under German auspices. All other political parties in Ruthenia were suppressed, and a successful election, with only the Ukrainian faction on the ballot, was promptly put through. The O.U.N. was particularly active in organizing military units and even in launching provocative attacks on Hungarian territory. Leaders of both the Magyar and the Ruthene groups in Ruthenia kept appealing to Budapest, and in March 1939, at the time of the German *coup* in Bohemia-Moravia and Slovakia, the Hungarian army moved in and took over the little Subcarpathian area. The armed Ukrainian minority put up a staunch but unavailing fight and the region was duly incorporated in Hungary on an autonomous basis. The Ukrainian literary language, as an obvious vehicle of irredentist propaganda, has been suppressed in the schools, and has been replaced by the indigenous Ruthenian dialects.

Throughout Eastern Europe, however, the Ukrainian Question still remains today's greatest unsolved problem in nationality. There has thus far been a fatal lack of unity of purpose as between Communists, monarchists, terrorists, and constitutionalists; there has been a lack of sane and educated leadership; there has even been a lack of national self-consciousness throughout large Ukrainian-speaking groups. The potent ferment of nationalism is at work, however, and it is hard to envisage any permanent solution of East European politics that does not permit a reasonable realization of Ukrainian nationhood. For the moment, the overwhelming majority of the Ukrainians are under the domination of Moscow; but Moscow is ruthless towards any effective stirrings of nationalism. Possibilities in the future are: (1) ultimate disappearance through the solvent action of Communist repression and education (a Moscow version, to be offset by the bitterly persistent power of the nationalist spirit); (2) the creation of a Ukrainian vassal state by a victorious Hitler (a Berlin version, to be offset by the chances of Hitler's defeat); (3) the gradual toleration of national home rule, after long years, in a mellowing U.S.S.R. (an historical forecast, based on the evolutionary analogies of the French revolution, but offset by the disruptive possibilities of our times); and (4) a limited sovereignty in a United States of Europe, conceding large measures of local autonomy but pooling the economic and higher political interests of the Continent (a possible Allied reconstruction programme, offset by the inveterate forms of jealousy, pride, and short-view self-interest to which human nature is prone).

The sudden Russian seizure of Eastern Poland in September 1939 has altered the whole situation. On the pretext of "protecting" the White Ruthenian and Ukrainian population, but really to protect the interests of the U.S.S.R. from too extensive a Nazi advance, the whole country from Bialystok and Przemysl east, containing upwards of 5,000,000 Poles, along with the other nationalities, has been taken over and is being organized into a couple of Communist republics, one White Ruthenian and the other Ukrainian. This not only means the segregation and probable extermination of the Polish upper and middle classes, along with the intelligentsia and the clergy. It will almost certainly mean a similar fate for the Ukrainians of the same categories. The Ukrainian nationalist movement in Poland has never had a strong or successful Communist phase, and the advent of Soviet control will tend to mean the extinction of the indigenous Ukrainian nationalism rather than its liberation.

CHAPTER VIII

RUSSIA AND ITS NEIGHBOURS

THE announcement in August 1939 of a definite pact between Moscow and Berlin brought headaches and bewilderment to those numerous optimists who had been hoping confidently for a Franco-British-Russian alliance to restore the Balance of Power and to supply the foundation for a rehabilitated League of Nations. It was obvious that the territories of the U.S.S.R. were the coveted objective of Hitler's Eastern Policy, and it had therefore been assumed that out of simple self-interest the Soviet government would align itself with Britain and France to check the *Drang nach Osten*. It was significant, however, except to those who willed to disbelieve, that at the Communist Congress held in Moscow in March 1939 responsible leaders openly declared that they had no intention of being trapped into participation in a "capitalistic war", but that they would hope rather for a triumph for World Communism to emerge in due season from such a war. "The principal task of party members," said Stalin on that occasion, "ought to be to facilitate the explosion of the general war. The direct resumption of an extension of revolutionary action will be possible only if we succeed in exploiting the antagonisms between the capitalistic states in order to plunge them into an armed struggle amongst themselves." It begins to look as if Stalin were the shrewdest poker-player of them all. He has obviously counted on the certainty that the Poles would fight and that the capitalistic states (France, Britain, Poland,

Germany, and perhaps Italy) would therefore engage in a struggle so terrific and so evenly matched as to leave them shattered and exhausted—and hence ripe for revolution and the fruitful intervention of the world's largest army. In the meantime, moreover, his freedom from a German threat would compel the Japanese to walk softly in the Far East; and would, by the very fact of a Russo-German accord, throw the anti-Comintern group into embarrassed confusion. Japan's *volte-face* and the hesitating neutrality of Italy and Spain were no doubt partly caused by this stroke of diplomacy.

The subsequent aggressive action by the Soviet army and diplomatic service, has confirmed these earlier alignments. The Berlin-Rome Axis, as a Siamese twin of the Anti-Comintern Pact, died quietly when the latter was murdered. The devout Catholicism of the Poles who have been savagely conquered by Hitler, and of the Poles and Uniate Ukrainians now being submerged in Communism by Stalin as a result of the Russo-German alliance, has alienated whatever good will either the Catholic Italians or the Catholic Spaniards may have had for the Third Reich, once the sworn foe of their bogey, the Red Beast of Muscovy. The expulsion of German commercial agents from Spain is already in full swing.

The true meaning of Stalin's sudden co-operation with Hitler is not easy to fathom. The ideologies of the two régimes had been utterly antagonistic, and each had posed as the world's chief champion against the menace of the other. The motives of Hitler, in wanting to avoid encircle-ment, and to face only one set of adversaries at a time, are cynical as to philosophical principles but convincing as Bismarckian tactics. If he can only settle with the West, by war or diplomacy, he can then get his second wind and turn to his long declared major objective, the conquest of Russia. The motives of Stalin are less clear, but may be suspected. In his speech at the recent Communist Congress, quoted above, he urged the avoidance of entanglement in a general war, while favouring the outbreak of such a war between capitalist nations only. Stalin has for years suspected the British of seeking to involve Russia in a war with Nazidom, whereby, as a result, the full force of German aggression would be expended in Eastern Europe, leaving Britain and France relatively unharmed. In the light of that suspicion, he refused to commit himself to an anti-Hitler bloc that might have brought him into war. It has been plausibly argued that he believed a friendly pact between himself and Hitler would actually turn the tables on the Franco-British schemers and encourage Hitler in such predacious designs against Poland as would force the French and British, if they were really serious, to defend the Poles by a major war—seriously weakening both to Germany and to the Allies. The occupation of Eastern Poland by Soviet troops need not have been pre-arranged, and there is much evidence to show that it caught the Germans entirely by surprise; but in any case, granted the lightning success of the Nazi troops and the hasty withdrawal of the Polish government, it was only a matter of elementary self-defence for Russia to occupy Eastern Poland and keep the Germans at a distance from the Galician oil-fields and the frontiers of Rumania and the Ukraine.

Even yet the strategy of the Allies, who neither sent an air-fleet to Poland, nor bombed the industrial centres of Germany, nor even attacked the German frontier in force, has not convinced the Russians that Britain and France mean business. Stalin does not want war, and he trusts no

one—certainly not Hitler. Aggressive Russian action during a time of opportunity has therefore been devoted to
strengthening the Soviet position along the entire western
frontier from Finland down to Turkey. Strategic concessions are being extorted, under pressure, from the Baltic
states—concessions which can envisage no effective adversary other than Germany. In mid-Poland there is
indeed the new hazard of a common frontier with Germany, but the vital centres of the U.S.S.R. are thereby
made more remote from attack. In the Eastern Beskids,
the Russian frontier forces constitute a direct threat on the
flank of Hungary in the passes of Hungarian Ruthenia,
thereby warning off any unsanctioned attack on Rumania.
All through the Balkans, Russian prestige has grown im-
measurably; and Turkish policy at the Straits includes
Russia as a major factor.

Russian military action on Germany's side against
France and Britain is scarcely credible. In view of Hitler's
known estimate of Communism and the existence of millions of suppressed German Communists as the chief revolutionary threat within the Reich, the Nazis are scarcely
likely to invite Soviet troops, or even the Red Air Force,
to join them on German soil. Many Russian Communists
are actually prophesying an early and successful Communist revolt in Germany, to which Moscow would then
be prepared to give assistance; but all that may be wishful
thinking on their part. There remains a grave danger, however, that if Nazi Germany breaks under Allied pressure,
before or after an unsuccessful Blitzkrieg in the West, it
will swing violently in the direction of Communism, with
some risk of a partial infection in the armies of France.
The influence of Soviet Russia is thus far-reaching in its
potentialities.

THE BALTIC STATES

Lying north of Poland, between the U.S.S.R. and the Baltic Sea, are three small republics: Lithuania, Latvia, and Estonia. While their combined area is roughly 65,000 square miles, or about that of England plus Wales, their combined population is only five and a half millions, or about that of medieval England. The countryside is comparatively low and level, and the glacial soil is often very fertile. Large areas are still undeveloped, and the region is therefore regarded by German expansionists of the *Lebensraum* school as specially adapted for colonization.

The Estonians and Latvians (Letts) had never known nationhood prior to 1918. Their earliest conquerors had been the Danes, but effective colonization was carried out by the Teutonic Knights, who converted the inhabitants to Christianity and made them their serfs. Sweden later assumed control of most of this area in the seventeenth century. Owing to the successive influence of Germans and Swedes, the Estonians and Letts are mostly Lutheran in faith. Lithuania had an independent existence in pagan times, but after union with Poland by royal marriage in 1386 and by statute in 1569, its identity was lost in the higher culture of the Polish state, and its religious faith, in contrast to the Protestantism of the Estonians and Letts, became permanently Roman Catholic.

In the eighteenth century, these areas passed under the control of Tsarist Russia and a ruthless campaign of Russification ensued. In the later nineteenth century, partially as a result of encouragement from a Government that sought thus to counteract German influence in the north and Polish stirrings in the south, nationalist movements arose among the Estonians, Letts, and Lithuanians, which exploded violently but unsuccessfully in 1905.

The emergence of three independent Baltic states was made possible only by the break-up of the German and Russian empires through the Great War. The Germans occupied Lithuania in 1915, and by 1917 had over-run Latvia and Estonia as well. Requisitioning and terrorization were ruthless, yet the German occupation probably saved these regions from being engulfed in the Soviet Union in 1917. The defeat of Germany in 1918 led to its evacuation of the Baltic littoral. There was an ensuing Bolshevik invasion, but the nationalist armies of the little peoples themselves, aided under varying circumstances by Germans, the White Russian Army of Yudenich, the Poles, and an Allied Military Mission, succeeded in an ultimate vindication of their independence in 1920.

Lithuania, with 2,500,000 inhabitants, has the largest population of the three. The Lithuanian language is an archaic Aryan tongue related to the Slavic group. The capital, Kaunas, is about the size of Ottawa. Lithuanians constitute 84 per cent. of the population; and the chief minorities are Jews, Poles, Russians, and Germans. Virtual dictatorship has been in force for the past thirteen years, and the minorities have been badly treated.

Latvia, with a population of 2,000,000, is the second largest Baltic state. The capital, Riga, is a seaport with a population (385,000) comparable to that of Vancouver. The Letts, whose language is closely akin to Lithuanian, constitute 80 per cent. of the population, the next largest groups being Russian, Jewish, German, and Polish. The minorities were well treated for several years, but the nationalist dictatorship in control since 1934 has been vigorously repressive, especially towards the Germans.

Estonia has only 1,126,000 inhabitants, 88 per cent. of whom speak Estonian, a Turanian language whose nearest relations are Finnish and Magyar. Tallinn, the capital, with a population of 140,000, is thus rather more than twice the size of Halifax, N.S. In the educational and cultural field, the treatment of minorities has been excellent and worthy of all praise. The political life of the little country has, however, been stormy; and since 1934 a corporate one-party government of a Fascist type has been in control.

By their situation, the three Baltic states form a buffer between the Third Reich and the U.S.S.R. The Germans are keenly interested in them, partly through historic sympathy for the German minorities, who had occupied a dominating cultural and landholding position for 700 years, partly because of the possibilities for extensive German colonization, and above all as a strategic area for dominating the Baltic Sea and attacking the U.S.S.R. The Soviet Union likewise covets these former Russian provinces for the dominating access to the Baltic that they would provide, and several attempts have been made (*e.g.* the Communist *putsch* in Estonia in 1924) to regain possession. In all these three countries, there have been very extensive expropriations of big estates (largely those of the German gentry in Latvia and Estonia and of the Polish gentry in Lithuania) for distribution among a land-hungry peasantry. The result has been to strengthen greatly the conservative forces in these states, through the disinclination of the very numerous new landholders to risk the communization of their farms at Communist hands. At the same time, they are opposed to any restoration of land, through Nazi support, to the old Germanic gentry, or to the importation of German farm-colonists from the Reich.

For the moment, Poland is the immediate object of aggression, but Poland is gravely overpopulated already and its subjugation can offer little hope for German racial expansion. Not so with the thinly inhabited Baltic areas, of which Herr Rosenberg, one of Hitler's closest advisers, is a native. As a first step, the recovery of Memel from Lithuania, along with most of the little republic's industries, places the Lithuanians pretty much at the mercy of the Nazis.

During the summer of 1939, the Baltic states were subject to a good deal of pressure to accept a guarantee of their independence by Britain, France, and the U.S.S.R. This they resolutely refused to do, and the British government was naturally reluctant to force a guarantee upon them. The crux of the issue was the unwillingness of the little states to leave to the U.S.S.R. the decision as to what constituted German aggression and hence justified their strategic occupation of the Baltic littoral, for in that case Moscow might seize any pretext for such an occupation and then refuse to withdraw.

I have recently visited all of the European countries adjacent to or near the U.S.S.R., and it is my impression that the governments of all these countries, anxious as they are to resist German aggression, would rather be conquered by the Nazis than "saved" by a Soviet army. Rightly or wrongly, they believe that the latter experience would sooner or later mean the setting up of Communist régimes, the annihilation of the middle and upper classes, the extermination of religion, and the liquidation of all property, even that of the peasants.

CHAPTER IX

THE REMAINING NEUTRALS

(i) HOLLAND AND BELGIUM

EVERY Nazi handbook of geography stresses the necessity of Germany's control of the mouth of "the German Rhine"; and the Nazis regard both the Dutch and the Flemish (whose languages are really Low German dialects that have developed into separate literary languages in independent states) as "lost tribes" that need to be restored to the ancient Motherland. Holland and Belgium are therefore, on general principles, in danger of aggressive action, not only as Germanic states to be reclaimed for Grossdeutschland, but as flank approaches to the more vulnerable side of France, and as air and naval bases controlling England.

In Holland, with its confirmed Calvinism and a long, splendid, fully-developed, self-conscious national tradition of its own, there is a deep-seated suspicion of Germany, like that of the old-line native-born Ontario Conservative towards the United States. There are no fundamental cleavages in the population, and the only German attempt at interference has been the formation of a Dutch Nazi party, which came to grief at the last Parliamentary elections. What the Dutch fear is rather a direct conquest by the armies of the Reich.

In Belgium, Nazi peace-time penetration has been much more successful. The parliamentary system in Belgium has not functioned well, because of a deadlock among three antagonistic parties, no one of which is ever strong enough to form a Government and deal resolutely with the country's economic difficulties. A Fascist "Rexist" movement, on the orthodox Nazi model, developed phenomenally in the French-speaking part of the country during the slump and was distinctly pro-German. Mainly pro-German likewise has been the Flemish Nationalist movement, nourished by the rise to a majority position of the Flemish-speaking population. This group had long been treated as an inferior race by the French-speaking Belgians, or Walloons, but a higher Flemish birth-rate has enabled them first to equal and now to outnumber the Walloons; and long rivalry has evoked an intense spirit of nationalism that threatens the very integrity of Belgium as a unified state. The Flemish nationalists do not share the Nazi view that they are really Germans; but they represent an instrument that might well lend itself to a German domination of Belgium and even to co-operation with Germany in an attack on France. Denunciation by Belgium in 1936 of its alliance with France was a natural result of these pro-German developments within the Belgian nation itself.

(ii) SWITZERLAND

Some 70 per cent. of the population of Switzerland speaks German. On that basis, the Nazis of Germany claim the right to annex the greater part of the Swiss Republic. As a means towards preparing for an Anschluss by conquest, Austrian-style, they have been organizing and financing a German Nazi movement in Switzerland. This is Nazi mysticism at its worst. The United States of America speaks English, and on this basis, in keeping with Nazi argument, England would have the right to annex the U.S.A. to the British Empire. The roots of American indignation at any such proposal would go back merely to

1776 and the Revolutionary War. The tradition of Swiss independence, on the contrary, goes back six centuries and is far more profoundly felt than that of the United States. Swiss fear and anger are therefore at white heat today, both at the open Nazi threats to their liberties and at the Nazi attempts to create parties of disruption within the country.

(iii) SCANDINAVIAN STATES

Nervously poised on the northern fringe of the mael-strom are five small Scandinavian states that are desperately anxious to preserve their neutrality and their independence. Denmark, Iceland, Norway, Sweden, and Finland have been conspicuously successful democracies; but almost all of them have good reason to fear Germany, for the Nazi programme includes their absorption or their vassalage. Hitler covets Denmark not merely for her dairy produce but also for her strategic command of the Sound, dominating the Baltic and permitting (in Nazi hands) direct pressure on Sweden. Iceland has been asked for air bases on a strategic route to North America; Norway's ships and lumber would be an asset to any empire; and Sweden's iron ore is of vital importance to the German military machine, at least until the conquest of the Ukraine has been completed. In the case of Finland, Hitler seeks, by controlling and fortifying the Aaland Islands, to bottle up Russia's Baltic fleet in the Gulf of Finland. Finland itself would likewise make an excellent base for a direct land attack on Russia.

Nazi efforts to control these countries have met with varying success. In Denmark, the standard Nazi technique of financing a native Nazi party succeeded in electing only three members at the 1939 Parliamentary elections. Denmark is defenceless and weak, however, and has been bullied unmercifully in recent years, until the Nazis virtually exert indirect control over the Danish press. Nazi agitation in North Slesvig, ceded to Denmark by an overwhelming plebiscite vote in 1919, also keeps the Danes in a state of nerves. Iceland, protected by its remoteness and the interests of the British fleet, has peremptorily refused the German demand for air bases. Sweden, with a population of 6,000,000 is the largest of the Scandinavian nations. There is no German minority, and the country is open to German attack only by sea or through neighbours now neutral. German propaganda has had little effect on the Swedes, who have armed heavily for self-defence. In semi-Scandinavian Finland, however, the Extreme Right has always been strongly pro-German, ever since German intervention in 1918 helped to overthrow the Finnish Reds. Nazi attempts to back a Finnish Fascist party, the "Lapua party", almost succeeded in 1932 and again in 1935, but the Nazis overplayed their hand and a projected *putsch* collapsed miserably. The proposed fortification of the Aaland Islands by Finland in 1937 was directed against Germany rather than Russia.

(iv) ITALY

The strategic position of Italy has become increasingly precarious. Up to 1938, her position as against ultimate German domination was safeguarded by Catholic Austria and Catholic Hungary as her Danubian bastions, by the strength of strongly anti-German Czechoslovakia, and by the friendship of Catholic Poland. Behind this barrier to German eastward aggression, the Italians enjoyed widespread influence in the Balkans. With the German seizure of both Austria and Czechoslovakia, the indirect Nazi control exerted over Hungary, and the savage conquest of Poland, Italy's chief buffers against German force were rudely stripped away. The occupation of Albania last spring represented, in part, a move to reinforce her waning power in the Balkans, while the recent forced repatriation of Tyrolese Germans to the Reich appears as a desperate attempt to remove betimes a grave excuse for German intervention in Italy. Even in Spain and in the Arab world there were, until recently, signs that the Germans had been squeezing out the Italians as backers of the local nationalist movements, while the Italian adventures in Ethiopia and Spain have greatly weakened Italy, to the benefit of Germany.

While, therefore, the risks of the moment might seem to lie in the vulnerability of the Italian industrial districts, coast-lines, and lines of communication (especially to Ethiopia) to French and British attack, a long view on the part of Mussolini would seek to avoid ignominious vassalage to the Reich. Under the circumstances, complete Italian neutrality in the present European war would seem to be his likeliest policy, coupled with unmitigated opportunism as the tides of battle ebb and flow.

An additional factor, in the case both of Italy and of Franco's Spain, has been the shock to devoutly Catholic countries of Hitler's assault on Catholic Poland and his new partnership with Stalin. Nazidom's pose as the chief crusader against World Communism, supplemented by aid given, ostensibly against Soviet intrusion, in the Spanish Civil War, had led the Italians and Spanish to condone somewhat the persecution of the Church in Germany. Today, all that is changed; and Hitler, to the pious Churchman, appears in ever more lurid colours as a *Nero redivivus*.

PART TWO

CANADA FACES HITLER

CHAPTER X

ANGLO-SAXON AND FRENCH

(i) THE ANGLO-CANADIAN POSITION

THE five million Canadians of Anglo-Saxon origin represent in the main a projection of the character and traditions of the English, Scotch, Irish, and Welsh. Comparable to the Anglo-Saxon elements in the U.S.A., they are nevertheless much nearer to Britain in point of view, for nearly 30 per cent. of them were born in the United Kingdom and probably another 30 per cent. are the children of parents so born. Intimacy with Britain through trade and cultural contacts and through loyalty to a common crown has maintained in the Anglo-Canadians a much greater awareness of British and European issues than is common south of the Line.

In spite of a strong filial consciousness, there has developed, nevertheless, an increasing sense of Canadian nationality among the native Anglo-Canadians. The past two decades in particular have seen their earlier British Empire attitude yielding to a more purely Canadian attitude, sometimes isolationist and sometimes linked with a world policy of collective security, but in either case stressing the primacy of Canadian interests *per se*. It was in keeping with this development that His Excellency, Lord Tweedsmuir, on October 12, 1938, uttered his much quoted recognition of national principle: "She (Canada) is a sovereign nation and cannot take her attitude to the world docilely from Britain, or from the United States, or from anybody else. A Canadian's first loyalty is not to the

British Commonwealth of Nations, but to Canada and to Canada's King, and those who deny this are doing, to my mind, a great disservice to the Commonwealth."

In the face of the present Nazi challenge, however, all such distinctions have, for most Anglo-Canadians, little more than academic interest; for there is something approaching dour unanimity in their analysis of the menace of Hitler.

That analysis may be briefly summarized: The Nazi régime is based in Germany on a policy of terrorism and a suppression of civil and religious liberty. Stresses and seething forces within the unhappy Reich compel its government to seek ever new adventures in aggression in order to give some release to that national tension. While lacking a specific sequence of objectives, its leaders are yet driven to seek advantage in every possible direction. Naziism has thus become a dynamic revolutionary force, which seeks in every country, to the limit of stark possibility, (1) a mobilization of all citizens of German origin to further the world plans of the Third Reich, and (2) the stimulation and assistance of native Nazi groups, seeking to overthrow existing forms of government and to set up a régime sympathetic to Hitler. There is scarcely a country in the world in which some measure of this outrageous penetration cannot be proven; and Canada is certainly no exception. Not only have the Germans of Canada been subject to iniquitous pressure from the Deutsche Bund, the Deutsche Arbeitsfront, and the Canadian branch of the Nazi party, but there have been organized in Canada a number of Fascist groups, of which the "Blue-shirt" National Unity Party is the most specifically Nazi in type and affiliation. This group, which embraces both English and French, has claimed 80,000 members in Quebec and 12,000 in Ontario. Its Canadian

"Fuehrer", Monsieur Adrien Arcand, has boasted of his close association with the Nazi machine in Germany, and has talked freely of "the political march on Ottawa which will end up with power for us". The organization is semi-military, violently anti-Semitic, and anti-democratic. Its monthly paper, *Le Combat Nationale*, has been violent in its attacks not only on the Jews but on all of the duly constituted parties and institutions of Canada; but it has significantly disappeared since the outbreak of war.

Anglo-Canadians are thus convinced not merely of the iniquity of Nazidom and its menace to the world in general, but also of the specific impact of its ambitions on Canada and Canadian democracy. In the face of Hitler's effront-ery in proposing peace and friendship over the murdered body of Poland, the Anglo-Canadians, like their cousins in England, have no answer but one of dogged resolution in war. Not least in their grounds for opposition to Hitler's whole system is the mendacity of his record. A few of his falsehoods, all in keeping with *Mein Kampf's* deliberate recommendation (p. 252), may be conveniently listed:

1. In 1922 he voluntarily gave his word of honour to Minister Dr. Schweyer and others not to attempt a *putsch*. He broke it.

2. In 1932, he solemnly promised Hindenburg to sup-port the administration of Papen. He broke his promise ten weeks later.

3. He gave solemn promises to Kaas, leader of the Catholic Centre party, to set up a parliamentary com-mittee, including the Centre, to which the Government would be responsible. Instead, the Centre and other parties were suppressed by his Storm Troopers.

4. In the Concordat of July 1933, he solemnly guar-anteed to the Pope the security of pastoral letters, Catholic

schools and institutions, and the processions of the Church. All these promises have been broken.

5. In May 1933, as the new Chancellor of Germany, he solemnly promised all foreign powers that he would abide faithfully by the Treaties of Peace. He has torn them to ribbons.

6. In his proclamation of conscription in March 1935, he promised the world that the German army would never be used as an instrument of warlike aggression. He has used it to occupy Austria, Bohemia, and Poland.

7. On August 27, 1936, he signed the Spanish Non-Intervention Agreement. Three days later, large numbers of Nazi military planes began arriving in Spain.

8. On February 12, 1938, he reaffirmed to Dr. Schuschnigg, at Berchtesgaden, his full recognition of Austrian sovereignty, already guaranteed by treaty. Just twenty-seven days later, his armies occupied Austria.

9. On March 14, 1938, he assured Britain that he had no hostile intentions against Czechoslovakia. On September 24, 1938, he sent the Czechs an ultimatum demanding the Sudetenland.

10. On September 26, 1938, he declared that the Sudetenland was his last territorial claim in Europe, and this promise was written into the Munich agreement with Chamberlain, Daladier, and Mussolini. On March 15, 1939, he seized the Czech regions of Bohemia-Moravia and in the following August he began his swift and bloody conquest of Poland.

From such a man, promises imply nothing but the likelihood of their prompt and gross betrayal. Perfidy and cruelty stain his whole régime, from the sadistic Black Guards (*Schutz Staffel*), who dominate the secret police and the concentration camps, down to the lowest sneaking set of radio spies (*Funkwarte*). To compromise with them is to encourage them in their progressive conquest of the world. To be defeated by them is to suffer a catastrophe to all civilization. Such is the Anglo-Canadian version.

(ii) THE FRENCH-CANADIAN POSITION

The cardinal fact to be remembered with regard to French Canada is that its population is almost autochthonous and regards Canada (in terms of Quebec) as its indubitable homeland. While only 70 per cent. of the Canadian English are Canadian-born, over 97 per cent. of the Canadian French were born in the Dominion, and almost all of these, now three and a half millions in number, are descendants of some 15,000 French peasants who came out as colonists three centuries ago. This is *le miracle canadien*. During all the great changes of nations in the modern world, French-Canadian fecundity has been unremittingly winning for itself an ever-widening empire from the Canadian wilderness.

In character, they have changed very little through the centuries. They have all the incorrigible provinciality of the French provincial, and the same shrewdness, the same parsimonious thriftiness, the same indefatigability in toil. The pious Catholicism of rural France has also been transplanted entire and nurtured through the centuries by the sagacity and devotion of their clergy. In provincial and national politics, their chief concern has been for the jealous safeguarding of language and culture through the maintenance of "provincial rights".

Unlike the more recently arrived Anglo-Canadians and European-Canadians, they have few contacts with Europe and even lack in rural Quebec any real newspaper service to keep them in touch with the outside world. Their attenuated knowledge of world affairs comes to them largely from the radio and from the clergy. Under the circumstances, they probably know less about the world situation than any other group in Canada.

The years immediately preceding the present war found the Canadian French largely absorbed with a nationalist movement of their own, seeking a larger measure of economic independence for Quebec. Towards European affairs in general, little interest was shown, and judgments were largely made by a religious yard-stick. Franco's side in Spain had their complete support, because he was alleged to be the champion of the Church. Hitler's oppression of the Church in Germany was helpfully offset by the assistance that he gave to Franco. Catholic countries such as Italy, Hungary, and Poland were regarded favourably, while Soviet Russia, the exterminator of religion, was looked on with horror. The overtures of Protestant England to Soviet Russia, seeking to form a "stop Hitler" alliance, were roundly condemned, especially in so far as they might involve a Canadian entente with the Red Antichrist. On the contrary, the sudden, defiant alliance of Hitler with Stalin brought to the clergy, and hence to their parishes, a conviction that Hitler constituted a serious menace to religion and civilization; and with much sober head-shaking the conclusion spread quickly throughout the province: "Il faut arrêter cet homme-là!"

There have not been lacking those prophets of national disunion who have claimed to see Quebec as a fatally centrifugal force in Canadian life. These pseudo-Cassandras have received a startling set-back as a result of Canada's entry into the present war. At the outset, the absence of any serious French opposition in the Federal House to the war policy of the King government was construed by many as inconclusive, and there were grave fears that isolationist undercurrents were flowing strongly. A decisive test was promptly provided by Mr. Maurice Duplessis, the premier of Quebec province, who, with two years of office still to run, suddenly called for a new election on the issue of provincial autonomy. This he soon extended, in his campaign, to a virtual demand for non-participation in the war; and it was apparent that his victory would be construed throughout the world, and especially by the Nazi Department of Propaganda, as conclusive proof of the disintegration of Canada, the largest of the British Dominions. This challenge to Canadian unity was at once taken up by the French Liberal members in the Federal House of Commons, headed by Hon. Ernest Lapointe, who were prepared to stake their political careers on the issue of co-operation with the rest of Canada.

The result was an overwhelming vindication of French loyalty to the nation. In 1936, Mr. Duplessis's "Union Nationale" government had won 76 out of 90 seats in the provincial legislature, while the Liberals held only 14. In the 1939 election, on the issue of national disunity, the "Union Nationale" retained only 16 seats, while the Liberals swept 66. Quebec has proudly proclaimed to the world that it believes in a national unity wider than that envisaged by the strident isolationism of Mr. Duplessis and his kind.

Perhaps never before in the history of Canada has there been so inspiring and heart-warming a vindication of our integrity as a nation. It is evident that the will to unity is very real, and that the Canadian French are today ready to accept the good will of the Canadian English in a great common cause. Mere passive complacency over this result would, however, be a grave error. The reality of the issues that can divide and estrange us is no less real than before, and the time is ripe for a patriotic effort to face up frankly to these divisive problems of religion, race, and language, and to set them clearly in their subordinate place, as secondary to the ideals that we have in common.

These aims that can unify our national consciousness are at least three in number: (1) the saving of Christianity, as against that aggressive neo-paganism of Berlin and Moscow, which would destroy religious faith in order to exalt the absolutism of the State; (2) the preservation of civil liberty against the assaults of totalitarian tyranny, with all its bitterness of world-wide revolution; and (3) the maintenance of racial and cultural tolerance, as against the dogmatic arrogance and racial animosity of the Nazi propagandist. In the perspective of a world peril, the vast historical purposes that unite us overshadow altogether the issues that divide us. If the forces of nihilism conquer in Europe, what chance has liberty of mind or soul here on the North American continent? Even the United States, although it is still potentially the strongest nation in the world, would be no match for the armed transatlantic giant and could survive only in a permanent state of siege. Far from dragging America into war today, Canada is defending her essential liberties, and those of this con- tinent, from a world menace.

While too absolute an emphasis cannot be placed on these great ultimate aims in themselves, we shall also fur- ther their realization in a spirit of co-operative tolerance, if we remind ourselves more often that both French and British have already made contributions to them in the past. We too often forget, for example, (1) that we owe it primarily to the French, in 1775 and 1776, that Canada remained true to Britain, instead of joining the revolutionary movement of the American colonies; (2) that it was the French, in the Assembly of Lower Canada in 1829, who passed the first bill in any British legislature permitting a Jew to become a member of parliament; (3) that the uprising of 1837 in Lower Canada paved the way for responsible government; (4) that the French played a notable part in the founding of the Dominion itself; and (5) that 60,000 French enlisted in the Canadian Expeditionary Force, and that the number would have been far greater had not a Methodist parson been made chief recruiting officer for Catholic Quebec. On the other hand, it is well that the French should remember that the English in Canada also played their part in the winning of responsible government, and that, in spite of a widespread lack of cordiality and understanding, they have, as a group, shown towards the French minority's language, laws, and culture, a tolerance which, apart from Switzerland, is perhaps without a parallel in the world's history. We both still have very far to go; but the present realization of our unity of national purpose should spur us on to foster that unity in every possible way. And it may in the end paradoxically prove true that Adolf Hitler, without intending any such consummation, has done more than any other force in the world to make Canada a nation.

CHAPTER XI

THE EUROPEAN-CANADIANS

WITHIN the past forty years, a third great factor in Canada's population has emerged in the form of some two and a half million inhabitants of European origin who are neither Anglo-Saxon nor French. Few French or English Canadians seem to realize this phenomenal development, yet in proportion to our population we have more Germans than Poland had, more Jews than Germany, and more Ukrainian nationalists than Hungary. To express this by another yard-stick, we have nearly a million more European-Canadians than there are white citizens in the Union of South Africa. The Canadian Germans alone are more numerous than are the British in South Africa.

In Eastern Canada, the representatives of this third great group are chiefly engaged in urban industry but in the Prairie provinces they are both urban and rural. In the case of at least a dozen nationalities, the majority of the group were born in Europe and still have close ties of blood and culture. While most of them are naturalized Canadians, and loyal in spirit to Canada, it is obviously impossible for them to acquire an Anglo-Saxon's attitude towards Britain as a Motherland or to extinguish their keen interest in the European lands of their several origins. In their attitude towards the philosophy and programme of Adolf Hitler, the various groups, inheriting as a rule both special prejudices and special knowledge of European life unfamiliar to the Anglo-Canadian and the French-Canadian, react in ways that are different to both.

A survey of these various group-responses would therefore seem of great importance at the present time. The analysis that follows is based, for the most part, on a survey of the foreign language press in Canada for 1939. Inasmuch as war-time has resulted in a comparative unanimity of loyal support to the Canadian government, most of the illustrative quotations have been chosen from peace-time statements, which are more indicative of the wide range of nuances of opinion between these groups and even within them. In general, one may say that whereas the French-Canadians are far less aware of European issues than are the Anglo-Canadians, the European-Canadians are far more aware of them. In the main, their arrivals in Canada are more recent, their contacts are more numerous and vital, and some of their respective fatherlands are even more intimately involved in the catastrophic issues of peace and war. While some of the groups have been seriously exposed to the propaganda of Communism and Fascism, and a minority among them have even succumbed to such external pressure, the majority, by reason of these very attempts at penetration, are all the better aware of the challenge to democracy and liberty involved in the rise of Hitler.

While the European-Canadians surpass the Anglo-Canadians, and *a fortiori* the French-Canadians, in their awareness of European issues, they nevertheless resemble the French-Canadians rather than the Anglo-Canadians in the orientation of their loyalty. The allegiance of the Anglo-Canadian to Canada does not cut across his heritage of affection for Britain, and hence the two sentiments are so inextricably intermingled that he often cannot clearly

distinguish between the two. The allegiance of the
European-Canadian, like that of the French-Canadian, is
rather to Canada, *qua* Canada, without that affection for
Britain which is historically impossible for him and which
it would be hypocrisy for him to simulate. The two greatest
obstacles to our national unity will have been surmounted
(1) when Anglo-Saxons in Canada realize the fundamental
fact that loyalty to Canada need not (and for more than
half the population of Canada cannot) include *filial* affection for Britain and (2) when European-Canadians *as sons
by adoption* share the affection and admiration for Britain
that springs from a fair appraisal of what Britain has accomplished and could accomplish for world peace and the
security of democratic institutions were she given the
active support and stimulus of all those living within the
sphere of her protection in the Commonwealth of Nations.

(i) GERMAN-CANADIAN OPINION

The largest national group in Canada, apart from the
British and the French, is that of German origin. While
the 1931 census shows only a total of 473,544, an analysis
of the figures for such groups as the Austrians and Russians gives a corrected German total of 549,376.[1] At the
present day, the German-Canadians must be in excess of
600,000. Some 70 per cent. of them are Canadian-born,
while another 10 per cent. were born in the United States.
In character, they are among our best citizens. Their
freedom from crime, for example, while not so marked as
that of the Scandinavians in Canada, is distinctly superior
to that of all remaining groups, including the English and
French.[2] In their acquisition of English (only 2.7 per

[1] *Cf.* W. B. Hurd, *Racial Origins and Nativity of the Canadian People,*
p. 224.
[2] *Cf. Ibid.,* p. 165.

cent. non-English-speaking in 1931), they are excelled only by the Scandinavians. The settlement of Germans in Canada goes back to the eighteenth century, when King George's Hanoverian regiments and the German-speaking U. E. Loyalists from Pennsylvania laid the foundations of German-Canadian life in the Maritimes and Upper Canada respectively. Apart from a commendable pride in their Germanic past, these earlier groups have been almost completely integrated into the Canadian nation. It is significant that there is today no German newspaper in Canada east of Winnipeg.

In Western Canada, on the other hand, where the present centre of gravity of the German-speaking population lies, there are numerous German newspapers and the Germanic community is both complex and self-conscious. The great majority of these Western Germans did not come from Germany at all, but from Russia (Black Sea area, Volga colony, etc.), Poland (Volhynia, Central Poland, etc.), former Austria-Hungary (Galicia, Bukovina, the Banat, Transylvania, etc.), and Rumania (the Dobrudja), as well as from Eastern Canada and the United States. Back of the European immigrants lay a painful struggle against policies of assimilation on the part of the Magyar, Rumanian, and Russian governments. In the case of the 31,000 German Mennonites, Lutherans, and Catholics who have escaped to Canada from Soviet Russia since 1921, their experience had been one of persecution, plunder, murder, and unmitigated horror. They have seen their families shot by the Soviet police, their clergy killed or imprisoned, and their thrifty German neighbours sent to perish in concentration camps as "kulaks". With this background of a pre-war flight from assimilation and a post-war flight from destruction, the Germans of Western

Canada are inevitably interested in the preservation of their language and culture and profoundly hostile to that Communism which has trampled their Russian communities into death and misery. Only in this perspective of their bitter experience can their present attitudes be clearly understood. The anti-Communist pose of Nazi Germany prior to August 1939 was a natural echo of their own sentiments, and the stress of the same Government on race, language and culture made an obvious appeal. Nevertheless, as a survey of their press will show, there have been marked differences of opinion within the limits of these common attitudes.

The most widely circulated German-Canadian newspaper is *Der Courier* (weekly) of Regina, with about 12,000 subscribers, a very considerable proportion of whom are Roman Catholics. Partially influenced, no doubt, by the antagonism raised among this latter group by the Third Reich's persecution of the Church, *Der Courier* has held the Nazi movement at arm's length and has announced categorically that it repudiates any such movement in Canada and is steadfastly loyal to the British Crown. At the same time, it expresses natural grief at the anti-German tone that is found in so much of the Anglo-Canadian press:

During his trip through Western Canada, King George will also come in contact with the German element. He will find German-Canadians as his representatives in provincial governments and other public authorities; he will find German-Canadians strongly represented in business and industry and especially in agriculture. He will learn that the German element in Canada comprises an inseparable part in the economic and political life of the country and has contributed much to its progress and development. He will learn further that the propaganda of hatred that has been unleashed against the German stock in Canada is without any justification, and that in this German element he has loyal citizens, who see in the British Throne and the British King the visible head of the country and cherish and honour him as such.   (May 24, 1939)

Next largest among the German-Canadian papers is *Der Nordwesten* (weekly) of Winnipeg, with a circulation of 9,000. This is the favourite newspaper of the Mennonites. Unlike *Der Courier*, it was (until the sudden Nazi-Soviet pact) rapturously enthusiastic over Hitler's régime in Germany, as is easily seen by an editorial of January 25, 1939:

And now came "the happiest of all German years", as Propaganda Minister Dr. Goebbels has called the year 1938. It was, as he said, a lordly year, crowned, as has been no other, with victorious consequences.

In this past year there have "returned to the Homeland" the Ostmark, formerly Austria, with over 6½ million Germans, and the Sudeten-German districts with about 3½ million Germans. "Greater Germany", for which countless folk have yearned for generations past, became a reality. Therefore 1938 has been called "the year of fulfilment". "Greater Germany" is today, apart from Russia, the greatest and most populous state in Europe, since the struggle over Austria and the Sudetenland has come to a victorious end:

> Great Germany is now risen victoriously—
> Past is the dishonour and the disgrace,
> One nation, one empire, and one strong Leader
> Have rent the bonds of servitude!
> Victory in this struggle was won
> Through weapons of justice and righteousness
> In the hand of the Leader of the Germans.

What the future is to bring, we do not know. But with its great Leader, and with all the other eminent associates and assistants, the German nation, which has become truly united for the first time in history, will proceed securely and bravely on its way.

Let us hope that the editor is just as right in these words as he was in those with which, in 1933, after a visit in the old Homeland, he concluded an editorial in *Der Nordwesten*: "I came home with the consciousness that the New Germany, firmly grounded in the nation and under the strong hand of a far-sighted government, had entered upon a victorious resurrection."

Der Nordwesten was ready to provide a political philosophy for the totalitarian state:

> While in America the greatest emphasis is laid on the idea of *human rights*, in Germany, as the expression of other circumstances, men stress the idea of *human duties*. This is a fundamental distinction in politics and morals. The concept of duty expresses Germany's philosophy and view of life much better than the concept of rights possessed by individuals. "No liberty without obligation" is a German maxim that may be found in the great German thinkers, Immanuel Kant, Schiller, Fichte, Hegel, and down to the present day. . . . From the concept of human rights, one passes easily and naturally to democracy; while from the concept of human duties one comes without much indirection to the Leader-State.

At the same time, its editor was quite ready to echo the practical demands of the Third Reich:

> Germany once had colonies, and needs them today! Her colonies are in other hands, but Germany demands them back; she must have them, on grounds of national prestige, as sources of raw materials, and as space for settlement.   (May 31, 1939)

In spite of this quondam support of Hitler's Germany, *Der Nordwesten* has been neither anti-Semitic nor anti-English. Both of these additional qualities were found, however, in Bernhard Bott's *Deutsche Zeitung fuer Canada*, founded in Winnipeg in 1935 by the German Consul, Dr. Seelheim, and suppressed at the outbreak of the war. Thus, an editorial of January 4, 1939, entitled "The Great Lie", strikes the two targets at once:

> Germany has truly treated the Jews, who as parasites were devouring her very life, more decently than England has treated the Arabs, who are only fighting for their own land and soil. Germany treats the world more humanely than the democracies do. Our way for the removal of the Jewish parasites from Germany is more humane than the methods that England has used in her colonial history for the suppression of native races.

In a further editorial of February 1, 1939, Herr Bott again betrayed that anti-Jewish obsession which, to a native Scotch-Canadian like the present author, whose household and children are "100 per cent. Aryan" on both sides, seems morbid and fantastic:

We go further, and declare that the fight which we are carrying on benefits Canada itself, for we keep opening the eyes of still more citizens to the dangers which threaten not only the right and freedom of our German culture in this country but also the foundations of the Canadian constitution and the Canadian state. The Jewish world-enemy, that continually assails us and practises a silent but obstinate terror against everything German and everyone German and propaganda hostile to Germany with all the devices of falsehood and hatred, is also the sworn enemy of sound Canadianism. It stirs and bores at the roots of the strength of this country, while at the same time it seeks to make un-Canadian and anti-Canadian movements popular under all possible guises. We have progressed farther in our knowledge of these dangers, and from our rich political experience we are able to see connections between international affairs and national life that are unhappily hidden from our fellow-citizens. Thus our fight against the world-enemy and his perfidious, war-mongering efforts is also a fight for peace, order, and upbuilding in Canada, without it occurring to us to wish to engraft another political philosophy on the life of the Canadian state.

England was represented as a nation on the decline, whose only safety lay in a speedy and pacific understanding with the rising world-power of the Third Reich:

Therefore the Britisher, drawn in leading-strings by his press, must be stirred up to a new passion of hate against the "aggressor nations" in general and the German nation in particular. What fate the haters can conjure up for their Empire under the circumstances, the incorrigible war-mongers seem unwilling to make clear, because in them foolish passion drowns out the voice of reason. Were it otherwise, they would have to tell themselves that for an England that believes itself to be on the decline and destined to sink to the rank of a second-rate power only one hope can be given: An honourable and lasting understanding with National Socialist Germany, with a simultaneous return of the German colonies, which neither England, surfeited with colonial possessions, nor the British Empire, with its vast empty spaces, needs at all. (Nov. 16, 1938)

Within Canada, the *Deutsche Zeitung fuer Canada* posed as the boldest champion of the German language and German cultural rights, and has given what is perhaps the most categorical statement of the bilingual school issue:

If the French-Canadians hold fast to the right of bilingualism, which for them really signifies unilingualism and the ever wider extension of their mother-tongue, then, as a consequence, the German-Canadians must possess the same right. In provinces like Manitoba and Saskatchewan, where there are specially strong German racial groups, it would be no more than right and cheap, by a scrupulous extension of bilingualism, to recognize German and English as the two languages that have legal competence. If indeed each racial group has the same natural right for its language, then the German-Canadians have it just as much as the French-Canadians. German is at least as much a cultural language as is French, and is steadily taking the place of French as a world-language.

The language question will never die out in Canada so long as the hitherto rapidly increasing French racial group exists. For us, too, the language question must always remain a live one, because it is for us a matter of the confirmation of our German nature and our racial existence, and because there can never be any true equality of rights, in the sense of the much vaunted "fair play", so long as this question is not solved with justice for all.   (May 25, 1938)

Incidentally, this paper claimed to be the only veracious and unmuzzled newspaper in its constituency, and remarked sarcastically in an editorial of April 26, 1939:

If the *Deutsche Zeitung fuer Canada* allowed itself to be controlled, like the English-Canadian newspapers or like certain German-language newspapers in Canada, then everything would be fine and good!

In matters of foreign policy, Herr Bott vigorously seconded the wide-spread French-Canadian demand for a clear statement of Canada's right to neutrality:

If our French fellow-citizens press with vigour for a clarification of the neutrality question, then surely Canadian citizens of German extraction ought to send a similar demand to the Government and to Parliament. In the past, it has often unfortunately happened that Canadian-Germans, out of excessive modesty, have left the final decisions on fundamental issues of government and state to other citizens. In the future, we must advance from our retirement and be more active than heretofore in making use of our own influence on decisions of far-reaching importance. It is not enough to be adherents, helpers, and supporters of a Canadian party. Canadian Germandom has no need to play so subordinate a role. The Germans, through taking possession of the eastern part of the country, belong among the earliest colonists and pioneers. German blood has also flowed for Canada. German sweat has also fertilized the Canadian soil in Nova Scotia, Ontario, the Prairies, and B.C. There were many people of German extraction among the Loyalists. Extensive stretches of Canadian territory owe their prosperity to German diligence, perseverance, and civilization. These are historical facts, which we cannot remember often enough. But they entitle us to throw our German-Canadian voice into the scales with all our might, if so significant a question as the position of Canada in a future war (from which may God protect us!) should come up for decision. (February 15, 1939)

An editorial of April 12, 1939, entitled "Hands off Europe!", amplified the grounds for Canadian neutrality, and incidentally heaped scorn on the incompetence of the parliamentary democracies, who could not solve their own economic problems and yet reviled and attacked the successful authoritarian states:

The further nursery-tale of the saving of civilization from "barbarism" can be just as quickly dismissed. A government that in a few years leads millions of unemployed people back to work and bread and defends them from the last desperate leap into the chaos of Bolshevism, that inspires its citizens with new courage and joy in life, that works unceasingly for the upbuilding of a better and fairer country, assuredly does more for our vaunted civilization than do those political chatterboxes who cannot cope with the economic and social problems of their own country but only drivel about a "high standard of living", which applies only to a couple of preferred strata in society. All talk about "civilization" is senseless, so long as the material foundations of a nation are not assured by the ordering of all available forces. Civilization can rest only on a sound economic foundation and on a just social system. That the so madly decried authoritarian states, and above all Germany and Italy, have accomplished a thousandfold more for it than most democratic countries is no "propaganda" but simple fact. When, therefore, democracy and civilization are not seriously threatened, at any rate from the "fascist" side, why should cannon-fodder be recruited in North America for un-Canadian war-aims?

What has Canada to seek or to gain in such a ring? Would it not be a criminal folly to sacrifice even a single Canadian life for those interests that would set up a new yoke of Versailles after the old one has rotted and mouldered away? Therefore all wise Canadian citizens, who have kept a clear head in spite of hatred and falsehood, must rally together in a league of sound human reason against the dark forces of passionate belligerents, who without a doubt would once more lead thousands to the shambles, either to cripple them for alien and un-Canadian ends or to send them to their death.

If Canada is to fulfil its rights and duties as a member of the family of the British Empire, the government at Ottawa must address a powerful warning to London, a warning against any further peace-disturbing political adventures, such as in past years—to think only of the "sanctions" against Italy—have proved such a grievous fiasco.

Herr Bott specifically denied, however, that the Third Reich sought to undermine in any way the German-Canadian's political loyalty to Canada:

One point that must here, once and for all, be clearly and expressly set forth, is the relation of the German-Canadian to the New Germany. As the English-conscious Canadian citizen follows with vital interest the domestic and foreign politics of his British motherland, as the Ukrainian in Canada shares by propaganda, sacrifice, and recruiting in the struggle of his people in Europe for national existence, as the other national groups in Canada bring the keenest interest to bear on the fate of their ancestral stocks beyond the ocean, even so every single German-Canadian is stirred to the depths of his being by the mighty events in the Third Reich. That is a perfectly natural and (for every thinking man) understandable thing, for the voice of one's blood and the possession of a common mother-tongue are highly significant factors, which Liberal, Bolshevist, and otherwise internationally orientated fanatics gladly falsify but cannot thereby eliminate from the world. . . .

It was and is for the German people, always and everywhere, an obvious fact that we combine loyalty to the state to which we belong and loyalty to the nationality from which we have sprung and which we have to thank for our best essence. . . . We can state here with downright certainty that the Germany of Adolf Hitler requires no national connection with the German Reich from Germans abroad who are citizens of another state. That is expected only from Germans abroad who have remained citizens of the Reich. He who asserts the contrary, betrays either groundless ignorance or deliberate malice. That which has always bound us to the German nation, and always will bind us, is a community of blood, language, and culture. (February 1, 1939)

All this is speciously plausible, if read in a vacuum. The aggressive purpose behind it all may, however, be read in the *Deutsche Zeitung fuer Canada* of December 30, 1936, in the published details of a four-year plan for the Deutsche Bund in Canada, signed by Hans Grabowsky and G. Hittler of Montreal, the leader and secretary respectively of this new Nazi organization:

In accordance with the proclamation of *our Leader, Adolf Hitler* (and as implemented by Major-General H. Goering), we herewith make public the four-year plan of the Deutsche Bund in Canada. . . .

All parents who belong to the Deutsche Bund are obliged to send their children to German schools in order that the children may be taught the German language and German history. . . . The teaching staff in German schools is to be composed of National Socialists. . . . We impose on parents as a special duty that they send their children to the youth groups of the Deutsche Bund. . . . Every member of the Bund is to take care to buy newspapers, periodicals, and books only in stores that are openly friends of the Third Reich.

Every member of the Bund is to demand German goods at all times and in all places. . . . The greater the demand, the greater will be the increase of German goods to Canada, and hence more foreign exchange will be made available to Germany.

The four-year plan of the Deutsche Bund comes into force with this publication.

We command that the members of the Bund place themselves unconditionally behind their leaders in order that we may accomplish the task that we place before ourselves without any omissions. In this spirit we greet all the members of the Bund with Heil Hitler!

It would be reassuring if one could be sure that no Canadian citizen of German extraction had ever been allowed to join the Deutsche Bund. In the case of two other organizations in Canada, *viz.*, the Deutsche Arbeitsfront and the Canadian branch of the N.S.D.A.P., membership has apparently been limited to Canadian residents who are still technically citizens of Germany; but there are widespread grounds for belief that many German-Canadians have been admitted to the Deutsche Bund, whose leader, as is seen from the above quotation, is Herr Hitler himself, the head of a foreign state. For that matter, even legally permissible organizations of the non-naturalized Germans may be a cause for misgiving. By the 1931 census, only 47.1 per cent. of Canada's foreign-born Germans were naturalized Canadians, and the rest would therefore be eligible for the efficient ministrations of the Deutsche Bund and the Deutsche Arbeitsfront. If a similar proportion of Germany's population were made up of non-naturalized Anglo-Canadians (reckoned on a basis of Canada's Volksdeutsche), there would be 600,000 rigorously organized Anglo-Canadians in the Reich, sworn to aggressive action in obedience to an alien ruler. There was obviously a stark attempt to recruit and mobilize the Germans of Canada in the interests of Nazi penetration.

Closely associated with the *Deutsche Zeitung fuer Canada* is the recently revived *Alberta Herold*, a little bi-weekly whose opinions may be gauged by an excerpt from the issue of July 20, 1939:

If one follows the activity of the beclouding-machine that is openly and secretly working in the service of the policy of en-

circlement, one will soon discover, if one has a spark of human intelligence, that a new outburst of the notorious war-time propaganda is under way, and that steps have already been taken for
the beleaguerment of sound human understanding.

With the exception of a small Radical sheet, *Der Aufbau*,
issued irregularly and surreptitiously in Vancouver, the
foregoing newspapers comprise the German-Canadian
organs of editorial opinion. There exist in addition four
weeklies issued under church auspices but without editorial comment. These are the three Mennonite papers
(*Die Post* of Steinbach, Manitoba, *Die Mennonitische
Rundschau* of Winnipeg, and *Der Bote* of Rosthern, Sask.)
and one Roman Catholic paper, *St. Peters Bote*, issued by
the Benedictine monks at Muenster, Sask. While lacking
editorials, these weeklies abound in signed articles and
letters from subscribers, giving one an interesting cross-
section of community opinion. As might be anticipated
from their background of European experience, bitter
hatred of Communism colours all that is written. In the
case of the Mennonites, there is frequent insistence on
noncombatancy (*Wehrlosigkeit*), which is a cardinal principle of their religious faith. These same Mennonites have
also become fascinated by the genealogical researches of
the Deutsche Ausland-Institut at Stuttgart, and are keen
to vindicate and glory in the authenticity of their German
descent. (In this connection, it cannot be too strongly emphasized that *all* of Canada's Mennonites are German in
language and consciousness. The fact that their sect began
several centuries ago in Holland has led many Canadian
writers to think of them as Dutch. Their language
of the home is the Plattdeutsch, or Low German, of
West Prussia, while their literary language is standard
German.)

An illuminating outburst of discussion over the claims
of National Socialism was precipitated in recent months
by a warning against it, published both in *Der Bote* and in
Die Mennonitische Rundschau, by B. B. Janz, and declaring in part:

> Yonder in Germany, people are now National Socialists; and
> they expect that I, a Canadian citizen, who belong here to no
> political party, shall nevertheless, openly or secretly, avow myself
> a National Socialist. . . . Everyone who speaks German here in
> Canada (or in the U.S.A., Brasil, Paraguay, etc.) shall make his
> declaration according to the statute over yonder, shall be a Na-
> tional Socialist. That is treason! . . .
>
> The spread of such a position would work out catastrophically
> for our whole racial community. Be warned, O my people! Have
> no more to do with propaganda from over yonder! "O that thou
> knewest in this thy time the things that pertain to thy peace!"
> (January 11, 1939)

To this position, H. Goerz of Arden gave his almost unqualified assent, stressing the Mennonites' loyalty to
Canada and their sense of benefits received:

> We would indeed extend our understanding and sympathy to
> Germany, especially because we know Communism so well and
> Germany is the strongest bulwark set against it. But our loyalty
> and our heart belong to Canada. In the case of most of us Men-
> nonites from Russia, it was not Germany that saved us from Com-
> munism, but Canada, because it opened its door to us and offered
> us a home. And therefore we owe Canada our love and gratitude.
>
> But we don't want to love our adopted homeland, Canada,
> merely out of a sense of duty. When we consider that we enjoy
> continually the protection and frequently the assistance of a
> humanly friendly government; when we cast a glance at the
> cultural and religious life of this land, which, along with much that
> is incomprehensible to us, also shows much true, living Christianity;
> when, finally, we have the opportunity to steep ourselves in the rich
> treasures of the English language and English literature; then we
> soon find much that appeals to us and makes it easy for us to feel
> more and more at home. And we desire to feel at home at last, after
> all our wanderings and all our grievous experiences in Russia.
> (*Der Bote*, February 22, 1939)

C. G. Schmidt suggests, however, that the Third Reich is the world's greatest protection against Communism, and that similar preventive policies may be necessary in North America:

If, perhaps, all details of National Socialism are not congenial or intelligible to us, yet we know that this movement is the greatest bulwark against international Communism; and already, on that account, we, who have experienced Communism in our own bodies, are induced or even compelled to express the greatest respect for this movement, without thereby coming into conflict with our duties as citizens. It is certainly no task of ours to glorify a foreign party in the streets or to parade it with a "Heil Hitler". Such conduct is witless and dangerous for us.

No one thinks of importing pure National Socialism into Canada. But only a similar direction can give a halt to the drive of international Communism on this continent. Already signs of such a movement are to be seen here and there. Whether these forces will be concentrated in one of the parties already existing, or whether a purely anti-Communist party will arise, remains to be seen. But Communism will certainly not surrender of its own accord, and in fighting it our land has need of loyal citizens. (*Mennonitische Rundschau*, March 1, 1939)

C. Martens complains bitterly about the Anglo-Saxons' obstinate and fatuous refusal to face the facts regarding Russia:

Why is no one disturbed on account of Russia, where all Christian churches have been turned into cinemas, warehouses, and houses of ill fame; where Christ is most shamefully reviled as a bastard, God as a lecher, and the Mother of God as a whore; where family life has been destroyed, thousands of ministers have been sent into exile and others murdered by the G.P.U.; where Christian marriage has been abolished, and the whole Christian religion exterminated. . . . These are facts. Millions of innocent persons, who never came before a court, have been murdered by the police. . . . For twenty years this has gone on, and the best people have been destroyed. There sit the ambassadors of all countries and keep deadly silence about it, as if nothing in the world were happening. When in another country a couple of missionaries are killed, there are diplomatic activities about it; but when an entire Christian nation is destroyed, nothing unusual is happening!   (*Mennonitische Runds-chau*, March 29, 1939)

Julius Heinrichs, in urging that German-Canadians should join the Deutsche Bund, seeks to justify such an organization as revealing the Communist menace and as defending the German name and German culture:

> A Christian who is a good citizen of his state will also be a loyal member of his race. If a spiteful press assails his race with lies and dirt, he will not restrain himself, but will freely and openly protect his race. In order to carry on this fight, men of like mind should band together and form unions and Bunds, which are permitted by the state. All who are of German origin and acknowledge themselves to be of German culture are welcome here. No compulsion! To be German and to remain German is the object. . . .
>
> If we wish to help protect the foundations of the Canadian government and the Canadian state, we must open the eyes of our fellow-citizens to the dangers that a bolshevizing of the world can bring.   (*Der Bote*, February 22, 1939)

Most extreme of all is Walter Quiring, who, after stressing the familiar distinction between state-loyalty and folk-loyalty, warns the Mennonite clergy that if they persist in opposing National Socialism's racial doctrines they will themselves be repudiated by the Mennonite laity in the day when Hitler's Germany conquers Russia and liberates their kinsmen:

> To everything that Herr Janz says with regard to our relationship to the non-German state in which we actually live, every German in the Reich will also subscribe. It is an error to assume that we here are of a different opinion. We Germans are a nation without sufficient space. Because we all have not places in Germany, 20 million Germans must live abroad. That these 20 millions ought to be true citizens of their foster-countries is self-evident to every man of decent feeling. It is an unfortunate error to assume that anyone in the Reich could approve of disloyalty of our people towards Canada. No, it is self-evident to every one of us that a Canadian citizen of German origin owes his loyalty, his state-loyalty, to Canada.

But there is still another kind of loyalty. There is not only a loyalty towards a state, but a loyalty, for example, towards God, towards one's wife, and towards one's own folk. These are not all the same. I can very well be loyal to the Canadian or Brasilian or Paraguayan STATE, and at the same time be loyal to my German NATIONALITY. In what does loyalty to one's nationality consist? In my having the courage honourably and frankly to say to the Englishman or the Brasilian or the Paraguayan: I will certainly always be loyal to the country in which I live, but I have no intention of becoming an Englishman or a Portuguese-Brasilian or a Spanish-Paraguayan. I intend to remain German, and I intend to have my children and children's children also remain German.

There is likewise an awakening among our [*Mennonite*] groups abroad. Those who oppose this sound development, and who are fighting against it by the most objectionable means, are over 90 per cent. preachers. . . . It is pardonable at the beginning to fight against this slow growth of consciousness, this awakening, and to withstand it. But he who attempts that, is fighting with bare hands against the wings of a windmill. I am afraid that our clergy, who have guided our little groups until today, will not recognize the signs of the times and will find no foothold in the entirely new age. At this turning-point, they will deny our history. Therefore they must not be surprised if, in a liberated Russia, we shall lay their dismissal papers on the table! (*Der Bote*, March 22, 1939)

It is evident that Mennonite opinion has been in a turmoil, and that National Socialism has been tending to split that religious community wide open.

When we turn finally to the Catholic weekly, *St. Peters Bote*, we find, along with an inevitable hostility to Communism, an implacable enmity for the philosophy and programme of Hitler:

If we reject and attack the false teaching of National Socialism, we are serving the German cause better than we could in any other way. *St. Peters Bote* is absolutely and completely independent. (May 4, 1939)

The ground of this enmity for National Socialism is not only Hitler's attack on the Church but also the dangerous

fate that Hitler's foreign policy seems to be preparing for
Germany:

> When, a short time ago, Germany's National Socialist Chancellor
> proudly rattled his sword and shouted: "Germany will never be-
> come Bolshevist!" and at the same time attacked the Church, the
> strongest and only reliable bulwark against Bolshevism, cutting off
> its rights and freedom and so renouncing the branch on which he
> and his German heroes sit, what is one to think of such a sequence?
> What is one to conclude regarding such statecraft? Of what use are
> all the armaments, fortifications, fiery speeches, and marching of
> troops? They merely evoke the same sort of thing, perhaps in still
> more gigantic measure, in mighty Soviet Russia. Through such
> means of force, tension, nervousness, discord, armaments, and
> threats of war are increased still more, until at last, as in June 1914,
> a spark flies into the powder-keg and is able to throw Europe and
> the world into a fearful chaos of war.

> One does not benefit the Fatherland at all by warlike tirades and
> insane armaments; and God will impose sure punishment on such
> arrogance, such proud dependence on one's own strength. (May
> 25, 1939)

It is even seriously argued in *St. Peters Bote* that the impending doom of Hitler's Germany will really be a punish-
ment inflicted by God for the anti-Christian activities of
the present German Government:

> England is seeking to draw a circle around Germany, and she
> will draw it. The word of Chamberlain, the man of peace, is sig-
> nificant: Germany will rue bitterly what has been done in her name
> against Czechoslovakia!

> Onno Klopp, a man who saw deeper into history than the end of
> his own nose, has written it as his weighty opinion that England's
> fearful policy of encirclement against Germany in 1914 was a pun-
> ishment for Bismarck's sixty years of unrighteous and unholy
> *Kulturkampf* against the Church. And today? What shall follow
> in the steps of Hitler's policy of hostility to religion and the
> Church? Is it again the fearful encirclement of 1914? (June 8,
> 1939)

The outbreak of war between Canada and Germany has
forced all these shades of opinion to a single focus, and

with the exception of the recently mobilized Nazi publications and organizations (now promptly suppressed), there has been a universal and categorical assurance of loyalty to Canada, a fact that it is well to emphasize.

Before the fears and suspicions of a war atmosphere have time to poison our minds, let us calmly remember that during the whole period 1914-18 only two thousand Germans had to be placed in our Canadian concentration-camps, and that of these over eight hundred were German sailors sent here from the West Indies for safe keeping. Of the remaining twelve hundred, arrested here in Canada, many were simply "unloaded" by municipalities who sought thus a cheap way of dealing with their indigent, and most of the rest were reservists caught trying to leave the country. In the present struggle, moreover, Germany is no longer the united nation of 1914, for large sections of German opinion repudiate Hitler and see in his defeat the only hope of peaceful liberty for the Fatherland. The growth of Canadian nationalism has also helped to cultivate a loyalty to "Canada at war" in circles that might, for historical and racial reasons, feel little sympathy for "England at war". On the other hand, a small resolute group of men have been definitely organized by Hitler's agents for penetrative action, and at these the Canadian police have struck with firmness and promptitude.

The chief German-Canadian paper, *Der Courier* of Regina, reiterates its consistent attitude of loyalty to Canada, and at the same time makes a very legitimate appeal to the Anglo-Canadian for considerate treatment:

In Canada live about half a million citizens of German extraction. Most of them are Canadian-born; a large percentage have been resident here for decades and have acquired Canadian citizenship. Although they have not forsworn their German origin, they have more than once shown their undoubted love for Canada. In peace, as in war, they never forget that they are loyal citizens of Canada, who not only enjoy all the privileges of a Canadian citizen but are conscious that they have also assumed all the duties that Canadian citizenship involves. (August 30, 1939)

While our duty will be fulfilled loyally, gladly, and freely, we have rights as well. And we appeal to the sense of justice and decency of our fellow-citizens of English extraction, to respect our rights as Canadian citizens. We are ready, in this serious hour, to do our duty, and we trust above all that the Government will place its full confidence in the German-Canadians, who have shown in the past that they are thoroughly worthy of such confidence. (September 6, 1939)

In the case of *Der Nordwesten* of Winnipeg, an earlier lyric enthusiasm for the Third Reich is suddenly hushed. With a strongly anti-Communist and Mennonite constituency, *Der Nordwesten* is apparently appalled at the new Nazi-Soviet Pact and openly renounces the Devil and all his works:

The "Nordwesten" has never had any connection with the Nazi movement. The best evidence for that is the fact that a new newspaper was established, which took the part of National Socialism and was on various occasions attacked by the "Nordwesten" because of its position.

The chief aim of Naziism was long the destruction of Communism. In spite of that, they did not hesitate to ally themselves with Communist Russia, and hence their earlier propaganda appears today as dishonest. In the whole course of history, there is no such alliance as that which has so suddenly emerged between two nations of such antagonistic views.

Poland's allies in her anxious struggle to preserve her independence are the great democracies, France and Great Britain. The civilization of the world and the freedom of its peoples is a worthy aim for this distressful time. Yes, it is worth fighting for, unless we are ready to spend our days under the heel of a tyrant. Since we know something about Naziism, Communism, and Fascism, we do not hesitate to say that all of these are unfit for Canada, and that the attempt to introduce one of these movements is a serious peril to the country. (September 6, 1939)

(ii) UKRAINIAN-CANADIAN OPINION

The Ukrainians are the fourth largest national group in Canada. Various exaggerated estimates of their number sometimes appear in the press, but the maximum official figure of the 1931 census, making every allowance for changes in European boundaries, was 244,629; and there has been scarcely any subsequent immigration. (*Cf.* W. Burton Hurd, *op. cit.*, p. 224.)

Politically, they are the most intensely self-conscious of all of Canada's minorities. It is scarcely an exaggeration to say that every Ukrainian-Canadian who is not a Communist is a potential Nationalist. This was not always the case, for in the great wave of Ukrainian immigration from 1900 to 1914 (when they were known to the Canadian public as "Galician", "Ruthenian", or even, quite misleadingly, "Austrian") a very large proportion were peasants with no political consciousness whatever; but the rise and fall of the Ukrainian Republic (1917-20) had an electrical effect on the Ukrainians in Canada, and a swarm of educated émigrés who came to the Dominion from Europe after the extinction of the Ukrainian state have astonishingly intensified, sharpened, and mobilized the Ukrainian-Canadian nationalist consciousness. The only comparable movement was that of the Irish Fenians in the United States in the nineteenth century; but the Ukrainian-Canadians are far better organized, more vocal, and more dynamic.

The majority of Canada's Ukrainians have come from the pre-war Austrian provinces of Galicia and Bukovina, today divided between Poland and Rumania respectively. In religion, they belong to the Roman Catholic church (the branch known commonly as "Greek Catholic" or "Uniate"), to the Greek Orthodox church, or to a schismatic nationalist derivative of the latter, known as the Ukrainian Orthodox church. Politically, they are Ukrainian nationalists, and are bitterly anti-Polish. The rest of our Ukrainians come from the Ukraine proper, and these are predominantly Communist in their sympathies. Canada has had virtually no immigrants from Subcarpathian Ruthenia ("Carpatho-Ukraine"), and hence the vexed question of that region is viewed only from the partisan standpoints of Ukrainian nationalism or of Communism.

In Canada, as in Europe, Ukrainians belong in politics to several conflicting camps, with consequently fatal weakness in their struggle for national independence. Their roster in the Dominion would include: (1) the Monarchists, the "Whites" of Chapter VII above; (2) the Fascists, a direct action sub-group of the "Pinks" in Chapter VII; (3) the Democratic Nationalists, another "Pink" subgroup; (4) the Uniate or Greek Catholic group, also "Pink" but without a political programme; (5) the Communists, the "Reds" of Chapter VII; and (6) the Russian Orthodox group, who, though speaking Ukrainian, have not developed any marked nationalistic spirit.

I. At the extreme right among the Ukrainian newspapers of Canada lies the weekly *Ukrayinskiy Robitnik* ("Ukrainian Toiler") of Toronto, which is not only Nationalist but also monarchist. For the throne of a restored Ukraine, it supports "Prince" Paul Skoropadsky, who was hetman or governor of the Ukrainian Republic in 1918, in the puppet régime set up by the German army of occupation, and has since resided in Berlin. The term "Prince", by the way, is meaningless except in potentiality, for historically the hetmanship never had any implications of royalty. The group supporting Skoropadsky are known as "Hetmantsi" or the United Hetman Association, and the *Ukrayinskiy Robitnik* acts as their official organ. Its editor, Mr. Michael Hethman, is a post-war émigré from the Ukraine. The headquarters of the United Hetman Association were long in Berlin, but have recently been suppressed by the Gestapo.

Up to March 1939, the *Ukrayinskiy Robitnik* was openly favourable to Herr Hitler, as the natural "liberator" of the Ukrainian nation, a man under whose auspices the Ukrainian state of the future would presently be set up, with Skoropadsky at its head. The "Carpatho-Ukraine" was regarded as the Piedmont of the impending national kingdom, and their enthusiasm was unbounded. All these hopes collapsed like a house of cards with the Hungarian occupation of Subcarpathian Ruthenia in March 1939, and their bitter chagrin with regard to Germany almost equalled their rage against the Magyars. Thus an editorial of March 24, 1939, under the heading "Hitler's First Blunder", reads:

The occupation of Czechoslovakia and the acquiescence of the Vienna arbitrators in the Hungarian occupation of independent Carpatho-Ukraine came upon the whole world like the stroke of a blunt axe. Without exception, the public opinion of all the world was stunned. No one had even suspected that such a thing could happen; and the reason why no one had ever suspected this was that the act was the very negation of that principle of the self-determination of nations that Germany had been propagating, as well as contrary to the ideas of Hitler's National Socialism, which forbids the inclusion in Germany of any non-Germans, and to the treaties of Munich and Vienna. . . . The fact that Hitler trampled under foot his own slogan about the self-determination of nations was a painful blow to us Ukrainians. It may thwart considerably our national aim, that is, the creation of a united and independent Ukrainian state.

Whether the Hetman Association would rally round Hitler once more, if given categorical guarantees of his good faith and support, is an open question. For the present, at any rate, they have been disillusioned as to his possible help.

Another factor that greatly complicated the foreign policy of this and the other nationalist groups, was the possibility of a British alliance with the U.S.S.R., compelling them, in case of war, to fight on the same side as their ancient and still implacable enemies, the Russians. Thus the *Ukrayinskiy Robitnik* wrote (May 5, 1939) at a time when Britain seemed averse to such an alliance:

> The British cabinet has decided, in its session of May 1st, that it would be harmful to Britain to come into direct contact with the Soviets and conclude a military pact. . . . We Ukrainians welcome the British decision, for if Britain had concluded a military alliance with the greatest enemy of the Ukrainians, the Soviets, then the Ukrainian-Canadians would have been placed in a most pitiable situation in being compelled to help the Soviets, the worst enemies of their national aspirations.

Somewhat similar in its orientation is the weekly *Kanadiyskiy Farmer* ("Canadian Farmer") of Winnipeg. It is privately owned by Mr. F. Dojaček, a Czech publisher and bookseller, and was formerly Liberal in politics; but its present policy is largely determined by its editor-in-chief, Dr. T. Datzkiw, an émigré graduate in law of Lemberg. Dr. Datzkiw's sympathies are with the Hetman party, but he does not regard his paper as being in any sense its official mouthpiece. The nature and extent of his recent repudiation of Nazi Germany may be gauged from a few editorial comments:

> At present, the German nation has few friends. In such a case it should have taken into account even the sympathy of the stateless Ukrainian nation. But it has happened otherwise, and so we must make far-reaching conclusions. (March 22, 1939)

> Under the influence of the propaganda of the German papers, a firm belief took root among Ukrainians that Hitler's Germany had a special interest in the Ukrainian problem and wished to solve it

to the advantage of the Ukrainian nation. That is why there was a general belief that the existence of the Carpatho-Ukraine was assured, because everyone believed that the Carpatho-Ukraine was only the beginning of the general solution of the Ukrainian problem, with the actual support of Germany. Now it appears that the belief of the Ukrainians in German support was built on sand. (March 29, 1939)

When the present dictator, Adolf Hitler, came into power in Germany, the sympathies of the Ukrainians for the German people did not diminish, and that for a good reason. The Ukrainians were not particularly fond of the Hitlerite regime, with its dictatorship by one man, but our people reasoned thus: If dictatorship is good for the Germans, there is no reason for us, who stand apart, to strive against it, as it is a purely German affair. (April 19, 1939)

The remarks of the official German papers gave us the impression that Hitler's government had really decided to come to the help of the Ukraine. Such was the general impression in the world; nor was it understood otherwise by the Ukrainians, who were glad that there was a Power in the world that understood the importance of the independence of the Ukraine. How, then, could anyone be surprised that the sympathy of the Ukrainians for Germany grew still greater at such a time? Our sympathy increased all the more because the democracies continually ignored us. Who could have suspected that the pro-Ukrainian propaganda in the German press was only a clever ruse to baffle the world? Who could have guessed that German diplomacy cleverly propagated the Ukrainian problem merely in order to worry those countries that had failed to find a solution for their own Ukrainian problem? (April 19, 1939)

As Dr. Datzkiw and most of his subscribers come from the "Western Ukraine", violent hatred for Poland becomes a major theme in the *Kanadiyskiy Farmer*, thus differentiating it somewhat from the *Ukrayinskiy Robitnik*, whose experiential background lies more in the Ukraine proper, where Russia is the villain of the piece. The following comment is typical:

Poland plays a game with the latest tragedy of the Ukrainian people, and expects that the Ukrainians as a whole, having lost all hope of German help, will throw themselves into Poland's embrace. This is a groundless supposition. The Ukrainian people in Europe would help Poland only in case Poland changed its methods of treating them from those heretofore in force. No one gains sympathy through pacification and the burning of churches, by means of the gallows and the gaol, by destroying the people's schools, by confiscating their land, and by similar brutalities. The fact that we have become unfriendly to Germany does not make us Poland's friends.   (April 26, 1939)

The war-time implications of the British guarantees of Poland were naturally a matter of grave anxiety to the *Kanadiyskiy Farmer*:

Herein lies the tragedy of our situation. On the one hand, a sense of duty towards Canada prompts us to defend it. On the other hand, the prospect of dying in defense of Poland is a horrible thing, and would be still more horrible because, by our sacrifice, we would be helping to enslave the Ukrainians living in Poland. (April 26, 1939)

II. Equally intense in its nationalism but unwilling to espouse the cause of Paul Skoropadsky is the semi-weekly *Noviy Shlyakh* ("The New Pathway") of Saskatoon, edited by Mr. N. Pohoretsky, a post-war émigré from Poland, and Mr. A. Hrihorovich, a former Alberta school-teacher. Behind it stands the Ukrainian National Federation of Canada, a modified branch of the Ukrainian National Organization (O.U.N.) in Europe, with headquarters in Jugoslavia. This latter group might be described as Ukrainian "Nazis", whose Fuehrer is Colonel Andriy Melnyk. In temper and programme, their patriotism is closely akin to that of the Irish Republican Army. They are anti-Semitic, markedly military, authoritarian, and anti-democratic in ideology, and had been outlawed in Poland for their campaigns of murder and terrorism. In keeping with this martial attitude, their Storm Trooper subsidiaries, the "Sitch" Guards, have been undergoing military drill and training in military aviation, with the specific intention of fighting against Poland, Russia, Rumania, or Hungary as the opportunity may arise. Since March 1939, they have repudiated Hitler as an enemy to their cause.

The aims of the milder Canadian affiliate will be made clear by quotations from *Noviy Shlyakh*:

> The Ukraine is passing now through a decisive period in its life. The Ukrainian nationalist movement has become in reality the only factor, acclaimed by the people, designed for actual struggle for the realization of national and social freedom. The new leader in the struggle of the Ukrainian people, the Organization of Ukrainian Nationalists, has decided to crush all the forces that occupy our territories and to build up an independent Ukrainian state. (March 23, 1939)

> Power, victory, and a great future will be secured for the Ukrainian people only by means of a nationalist revolution. (March 23, 1939)

> The nationalist and revolutionary preparedness and the readiness of every Ukrainian will show best in the final struggle. The appearance, extent, strength, and result of that struggle will not depend on the plans of Germany or of any other Powers, but only on the Ukrainians themselves. (January 19, 1939)

The range of their ambition, moreover, may be gathered from an editorial of April 17, 1939:

> The blood that was shed and the victims that fell in battle and through the firing squads and the gallows of the Finno-Mongolian invasion of March 1939, in the Silver Land (i.e. the Carpatho-Ukraine) are only a new investment in the treasury of the struggle for the formation of an independent and united Ukrainian state, stretching from the Tisza (in central Hungary) to the Caspian Sea.

Poland and Russia are alike monsters of iniquity in their eyes. As to the former, *Noviy Shlyakh* states:

> The attitude of the Ukrainians towards Poland, regardless of any international political combinations, cannot be other than hostile, since the attitude of Poland towards the Ukrainians has always been, and always will be, hostile. The Western Ukraine is waiting for the appropriate moment and the word of command to strike at the occupational force; and we believe that it will deal a mortal blow to the oppressor. (April 13, 1939)

After the gory incident of the Carpatho-Ukraine, a second heavy blow descended on the Ukrainians, when England assured Poland of its military help. This blow is most painful to us, here in Canada, not so much because this Anglo-Polish alliance is contrary to our faith in the international justice of British foreign policy, but because the Empire whose subjects we are has decided to give aid to a country that cannot be saved by any force whatever in the world.   (April 27, 1939)

Towards Communism, in Russia and in Canada, it is likewise very bitter:

In Canada, international Communism is waging a battle against Nationalism, *i.e.* against Canadianism.   (January 23, 1939)

We do not need to go outside of Canada. Let us take a look at the activities and the newspapers of the local Bolsheviks. It amazes you, amuses you, and disgusts you, when you listen to the sorrowful sympathy-seeking songs of the bloodthirsty Red sirens and see the alluring gestures by which, spider-like, they seek to ensnare the people in order to feed upon them.   (March 9, 1939)

Red Moscow has demoralized the League of Nations, and has created a political crisis in the world by its efforts to form "national fronts".   (May 4, 1939)

Our present democratic system in Canada it regards as hopelessly weak in its opposition to Communism, and it prophesies the possible triumph of Communism in Canada, unless its own recipe of authoritarian nationalism is adopted:

The Canadian "Kerensky period" of political emasculation may also result in a catastrophe as bad as that of 1917 in Russia. (January 23, 1939)

III. Still another group, opposed both to Fascism and to Communism and occupying a democratic middle position, is the Ukrainian Self-Reliance League. Its leaders have commonly been men like N. V. Bachynsky, J. W. Arsenych, and P. H. Woycenko, who have been educated in Canadian schools and colleges and feel that their first loyalty is to Canada. They have not renounced their

Ukrainian past and are keenly interested in the emergence
of a Ukrainian state in Europe; but they have always felt
that the Ukrainians should not look to Moscow or Berlin
for help. Religiously, they are closely related to the
schismatic Ukrainian Orthodox church. Their chief organ
of opinion is the weekly *Ukrayinskiy Holos* ("Ukrainian
Voice") of Winnipeg, edited by Mr. Miroslav Stechishin.

A comprehensive statement of its position may be found
in an editorial of January 11, 1939:

We are living in Canada. Many of us were even born in Canada.
Some of us were only brought up in Canada. Others have lived in
Canada for ten, twenty, thirty, forty, or even more years. Even
those who were not born here nor reared here from their youth up
have become so used to Canada that it has become their own
country. In most cases we are also legally Canadian citizens. We
are Canadians.

Yet at the same time we are also Ukrainians. We are Ukrainians
because our fathers, grandfathers, and remote ancestors were
Ukrainians. We have Ukrainian blood in our veins. Our past binds
us by invisible threads with the Ukrainian people and the Ukrainian
land. These ties are stronger than the ties made consciously through
one's own will. It is two thousand years since the Jews left Palestine, yet even now you can recognize a Jew at first glance. The
Jewish traits are marked on the Jew's face and in his character.
In like manner, we cannot obliterate in ourselves our Ukrainian
origin, even if we live a thousand years in Canada.

We are both Canadians and Ukrainians at the same time. We
call ourselves Canadian-Ukrainians, while the English call us
Ukrainian-Canadians. It is a moot point whether there is any
difference between these two forms of our name. Nevertheless, we
are nothing else but both Canadians and Ukrainians. From one
point of view we are Canadians, and from another, Ukrainians.
To a certain extent we are Canadians, and to a certain extent
Ukrainians; yet we are indivisibly both Canadians and Ukrainians.

And because we are indivisibly both Canadians and Ukrainians,
we sometimes face problems for which we must find solutions ap-
proached from the two viewpoints, Canadian and Ukrainian. We
must find one solution, though seeing the problem from two points
of view, for we do not want to divide our very entity, our own soul.

As is the case with all nationalistically-minded Ukrainians, *Ukrayinskiy Holos* is anti-Polish, anti-Magyar, anti-Rumanian, and anti-Russian. Towards Hitler, its attitude is one of ironic scepticism:

Hitler's policy is a very flexible one. What he has done to the Carpatho-Ukraine is not the Ukrainians' first lesson from him. God forbid that any more such lessons should come to us! (March 29, 1939)

The group represented by *Ukrayinskiy Holos* is anxious not to face a divided allegiance in case of war, and has therefore consistently pressed for a British policy in Eastern Europe that would safeguard the future of the Ukrainians. On the legitimacy of such pressure, the editor writes:

No one will ever forbid us, as Canadian citizens, to express our own opinions and wishes to the government of Canada, and through it to the government of Great Britain. Therefore we should not remain silent. To the question whether we must say something about ourselves to the governments of Canada and Great Britain, there can be only one answer: "Yes, we must!"

IV. Two Greek Catholic (Uniate) papers represent still another variant of opinion. These are the weekly *Ukrayinskiy Visty* ("Ukrainian News") of Edmonton and the semi-monthly *Buduchnist Natsiyi* ("The Future of the Nation"), printed in Yorkton. The editor of the former is Mr. V. Dyky, a graduate in law of Lemberg, while the latter is edited by Rev. Dr. W. Kushnir, of Winnipeg, a post-war émigré from Poland. *Ukrayinskiy Visty* is strongly anti-Communist, for it regards Communism as the deadly foe both of religion and of Ukrainian nationalism:

From the birth of the Carpatho-Ukraine until now, the Canadian Bolsheviks (*i.e.* those of Ukrainian descent) have stood in the same camp with the Fascist countries, Hungary and Poland, and (as a matter of course) with Moscow, against their own racial brothers, the Carpatho-Ukrainians. . . . Stalin's Canadian servants of Ukrainian origin have redoubled their stubborn and libellous struggle against the efforts of the Ukrainian people for freedom in Russia and Poland, two of the biggest forces of occupation in our land. These new Moscophils and Janissaries are so servile to their masters that even the alliance of Fascist-feudal Poland with Communist Moscow has made them glad.   (January 3, 1939)

Here in Canada, we are now facing a definite Bolshevist scheme; and so we, too, must have a clear-cut plan for self-defense. They want to take from us as many people as possible. Our duty is not to yield them even a single person. In order to counteract the Bolshevist propaganda, we must not only stand on guard against the Bolshevist attack but must also fight back against Communism. (May 2, 1939)

Buduchnist Natsiyi is also violently anti-Communist, but adds to this a bitterly anti-Semitic insistence that back of all Communism stands "international Jewry", seeking to destroy Christianity and to dominate the world. This paper is second to none in its nationalist consciousness:

Let us consolidate! Let us make use of all our possibilities in Canada so as to mobilize all our means under the battle standard of democratic principles, aiming to liberate the Ukraine! This will, at the same time, be an important contribution from us to the destruction of Bolshevism, the enemy of democratic Canada. (March 14, 1939)

V. Sharply over against all six of the Ukrainian papers thus far mentioned stands the Communist *Narodna Hazeta* ("The People's Gazette") of Winnipeg, the strength of whose following may be gauged from the fact that it is the only Ukrainian daily newspaper in all Canada. Its very competent editor is Mr. M. Shatulskiy and its general manager Mr. N. Navisivskiy, both leading Communists of Winnipeg. *Narodna Hazeta* openly proclaims Moscow as the source of all political and economic wisdom, but in keeping with the new popular front tactics it now invariably uses the phraseology of democracy. Thus an editorial of January 10, 1939, states:

It is not the investigation of Communist activity that the people of Canada demand, but the investigation of destructive Fascist (mainly Nazi) activity. The people of Canada stand for democracy, and oppose Fascism and reaction. The Communist party is the staunchest fighter for democracy, mobilizing and leading the masses of the people in their struggle against reaction and Fascism.

Towards British foreign policy, however, its attitude is that Britain is really engaged in a deep-laid capitalist plot against the U.S.S.R.:

The persistent aim of British diplomacy has been to consolidate the reactionary powers of Europe, to balance the power of France with that of Germany, and to turn Hitler against the Soviet Union. However, as a result of British diplomacy, France has become a second-rate Power, and in consequence Britain has become some-what isolated and has found itself embarrassed with regard to the Berlin-Rome Axis. Chamberlain and the British reactionaries dream that Hitler will turn his might (which has been augmented by Britain's capitulation) against the Soviet Union, leaving Britain alone.   (March 18, 1939)

Chamberlain has announced that Britain will give protection and aid to Poland, Rumania, Greece, and other states; but so far neither Poland nor Rumania nor any others have received any guarantees. Such a state of affairs makes one suppose that Chamberlain is not interested in the independence of Poland or Rumania but just wants to make them a redoubt for Hitler's attack against the Soviet Union.   (April 26, 1939)

Montague Norman and the international bankers have decided to give financial support to the aggressors, giving them the Czech money from the Bank of England.   (May 30, 1939)

The Government, the Party, and all the peoples of the great Soviet Union know that the Fascist incendiaries, together with the British Imperialists, are getting ready for a war by means of which they intend to seize the Soviet territory, together with its vast resources, and to re-establish the capitalist system there.   (March 15, 1939)

So far as Ukrainian nationalism is concerned, these Ukrainian-Canadian Communists have their own peculiar but none the less emphatic view of it. From their point of view, the people of the Ukrainian Socialist Soviet Republic are already enjoying complete democratic freedom, and only the minorities in Poland, Rumania, and Hungary remain to be liberated by a successful Communist movement. Obviously the sort of revolution that they favour would have nothing in common with the revolutions desired by the United Hetman Association, the Ukrainian National Federation, the Ukrainian Self-Reliance League, or the Uniate Church. For over twenty years, the friends and associates of these latter groups have been systematically exterminated in the U.S.S.R., and they know clearly what would happen to the Ukrainian nationalist leaders in Poland, Rumania, and Hungary if Russian Communism were to absorb these areas. Every Ukrainian community in Canada knows personally of men who have disappeared to the great penal camps of Siberia and the White Sea or who perished in the great Ukrainian famine of 1933, induced by the iron repressions of Moscow.

VI. The Russian Orthodox Church in Canada claims 100,000 members, most of whom speak Ukrainian and come either from Bukovina or the Russian Ukraine. This is the least nationalistic of the Ukrainian groups. In the past they have regarded themselves as a branch of the great Russian nation rather than as a separate nationality with an aggressive destiny of its own. Political consciousness beats very feebly in the Orthodox body, whose centre of gravity is in the great Vegreville colony in Northern Alberta. It has no press except the church publication, the *Canadian Orthodox Messenger*, of Winnipeg.

It will thus be realized that Ukrainian opinion in Canada is seriously divided. There is a fundamental cleavage between Communists and Nationalists; but even the latter, although they possess certain hatreds in common, cannot agree on a single leader in an active policy or even as to whether there ought to be an active policy at all.

The war with Germany finds all the Ukrainian-Canadians, both Communists and non-Communists, emphatic in their support of Canada and Britain.

The former had until recently been bitterly attacking Britain, France, and Poland for not forming a peace front with Soviet Russia on Stalin's own terms. This condemnation continued still more bitterly after the Russo-German Pact had allegedly demonstrated the essentially pacific character of the U.S.S.R. With the German attack on Poland, and the Nazi bombing of defenceless Ukrainian and White Ruthenian towns, resulting in the deaths of women and children, the Ukrainian Communist paper led the way in denouncing the aggressor and praising the Franco-British support of Poland. *The Narodna Hazeta* of September 5 states its case emphatically in an editorial entitled "For the Defence of Canada":

Such is the principle of the Nazi aggressor. The Ukrainian nation everywhere knows the price of this principle. They have paid for it with their own blood in Subcarpathia, they have paid for it with their blood everywhere in the Western Ukraine.

In the face of such a principle, our Canada stands firm. For the Ukrainian people in Canada one duty is sure: To stand in defence of their democratic Canada and their brothers in the Western Ukraine against the bloody Nazi aggressor!

The Ukrainian nationalists in general are vehement in their loyalty to Canada. Thus the Ukrainian Self-Reliance League, speaking through its organ, the *Ukrayinskiy Holos* of Winnipeg, states:

We are not authorized and therefore do not propose to speak on behalf of all Canadian citizens of Ukrainian descent. But on behalf

of the Ukrainian Self-Reliance League of Canada we are happy to
be able to assure everyone that all those many thousands of
Canadian citizens of Ukrainian descent who are members or are in
sympathy with the League and its affiliated organizations in
Canada,—*viz.* Union of Ukrainian Community Centres, Ukrainian
Women's Association of Canada, Canadian Ukrainian Youth Association (SUMK), with branches throughout the Dominion of
Canada, all those have never, at any time wavered in their loyalty
and devotion to the British Crown or to Canada and in their faith
in democratic institutions and that, therefore, all of them will
without hesitation respond to the earnest appeal of their King and
their Government and will faithfully serve and defend the vital
interests of Canada and the British Empire side by side with other
citizens by all means at their disposal and in every manner which
may be demanded of them.   (September 6, 1939)

Similar sentiments appear in the *Ukrayinsky Visty* of
Edmonton:

We, Canadian Ukrainians, as loyal subjects of Canada, await the
command of our government and stand on guard for our fosterland
Canada and the whole British Empire, by the side of other Canadian
patriots.

All our service—for the King, for Canada, and for the bright
future of the invincible British Empire!   (September 5, 1939)

And the *Kanadiyskiy Farmer* sums up its counsel thus:

Let us support our Government unreservedly and unconditionally.   (September 6, 1939)

In the *Noviy Shlyakh* of Saskatoon, however, the semi-
military O.U.N. cannot forget its bitterly anti-Polish
programme and urges that the Canadian and British governments must not be behind the Germans in their readi-
ness to "liberate" the Ukrainian nation:

The British guarantee to Poland in case of a German attack on
Poland was a very bitter blow to all Ukrainians. That step of the
British government aroused many Ukrainians so much that they
altogether ceased to have faith in the British good will towards the
Ukrainian cause. . . . In such circumstances we, Ukrainians in
Canada, can and must approach Canada and the British Common-
wealth of Nations, as we wish that they duly understand the cause

of Ukrainian liberation and duly work for it and keep pace with its development. . . . Is it not our civil and national duty to work for this as we worked before this crisis? Is it unnecessary? (September 4, 1939)

This point of view is steadily gaining ground amongst the other nationalist groups, and even leaders of the Uniate church have been urging enlistment in the Canadian Army as a means towards the establishment of a free Ukrainian state in Europe. As the *Kanadiyskiy Farmer* says:

We do not declare as yet that by shattering the German and Russian forces there will at once rise an independent Ukraine. But we are sure that victory over Hitler and Stalin will create a base for the Ukrainians to reconstruct a Ukrainian state. There is not the slightest doubt today that Hitler and Stalin are the greatest enemies of our aspirations and from this the Ukrainian people must deduce the farthest consequences. Events have come to such a pass that our state aspirations are bound up with victory for Great Britain and France and this we must not forget all the more, as our adopted fatherland, Canada, is a part of the British Empire.

The Russian occupation of Eastern Poland has been a great shock. The Ukrainian-Canadian Communists explain it as necessary for the protection of the U.S.S.R., which they still regard as essentially pacific in character, and they have jubilantly staged a five-day celebration over the setting up of a Western Ukrainian Soviet Republic with its capital at Lwôw. All the remaining Ukrainian groups are shocked and angered, however, for a perpetuation of the Soviet régime would seem to mean the extermination of all their European leaders and the extinction of all their hopes. The probable fate of the church, whether Catholic or Orthodox, grieves them profoundly. Word has already been received that large numbers of the Catholic clergy, including some visiting Canadian priests, well-known in Winnipeg, have been shot by the Russians in Eastern Poland.

(iii) SCANDINAVIAN-CANADIAN OPINION

The 1931 census shows 228,049 Canadians of Scandinavian origin, made up of the following nationalities:
Danes, 34,118; Icelanders, 19,382; Norwegians, 93,243;
and Swedes, 81,306. More than half of these were born
in Canada or the United States. In the case of the Icelanders, two-thirds were Canadian-born.

Just as the Scandinavian countries display in Europe
today what is probably the world's highest average level
of civilization, so the representatives of their stock are
probably the most mature and well adjusted democrats
that we possess. Significant as to their stable and law-
abiding character is the fact that their penitentiary record
is by far the lowest in the Dominion. The corrected rates
per 100,000 of population in 1931 (*Cf.* W. Burton Hurd,
op. cit., p. 167) are: Scandinavians, 29; German and
Dutch, 39; British, 47; French, 58; Slavic, 64; Latin and
Greek, 118.

Though their parent nations in Europe are not perhaps
very directly threatened by the Nazi *Ostpolitik*, their
opinions in Canada are not without significance for any
national alignment in case of war.

Our largest Scandinavian group, the Norse-Canadians,
are represented by two weeklies, *Vancouver Posten* of
Vancouver and *Norröna* of Winnipeg. The former has no
editorials, but the latter, edited by Mr. Magnus Talgöy,
is eloquent and incisive in its political comment. Take, for
example, its verdict on Hitler's Eastern Policy:

"The New Germany will not permit itself to be encircled, as did
the Germany of the Kaiser's day," says Hitler in a speech. That is
intelligently enough said from all sides. But that does not seem to
hinder the good Adolf from following exactly in the path that, with
its sterility of political stratagem, will result in Germany being
encircled and landing in the greatest catastrophe recorded by

modern history. And this is the man who dares to call himself the successor of Bismarck!

It is correct enough that Hitler is the greatest political genius of our time. And that he has accomplished more in a few years than others did in centuries, and that even Bismarck did not achieve so much. But now he has encountered that which gave the Old Chancellor the most hellish torment in his last years: the eternal German stupidity! The immutable stupidity of the German.

Adolf Hitler has opportunities that no one has had before him and perhaps no one will ever have after him. He has it in his power to settle up with the sins of the past and to create "Lebensraum" for 70 million stout, aggressive Germans in peaceful competition in the markets of the world. In good and normal commerce with England, the United States, Canada, and other foreign states lies more hope for Germany's economic soundness and future—both for the moment and in the long run—everlastingly more than some dream of a "place in the sun", situated in the Ukraine or elsewhere. But unless Hitler changes his tactics, his kingdom will fall as quickly back to dust as it has risen from the dust. But whether his glory lasts briefly or for a long time, his day of doom is certain. The New Germany bulks large and mighty on paper. But the German nation has been stripped naked, and there is no spiritual life left in it. This is more important for a nation than anything else—more important than Skoda Works, the Ukraine, the Corridor, and all that. For a country always stands or falls by the strength of its people's spiritual maturity. (April 6, 1939)

On the inner meaning of the Norse character, Mr. Talgöy writes:

We Norsemen do not have to speak boisterously about such conceptions as loyalty and co-operation. We are bred with that; it is ingrained in our flesh; but we cannot step forward in the market-place, thump ourselves on the chest, and burst forth in mushiness and tears: "Here am I, my lord, do with me what you please!" Loyalty, for us, has a deeper meaning. There is no real loyalty without social cohesion and well proven social life. Therefore, in connection with the question of the loyalty of any national group, the question of their social wakefulness must be raised. (April 20, 1939)

As to the service that a small nation like Norway (with a population no greater than that of Ontario) can render to the world, an editorial on "Spiritual weapons" expresses a clear-sighted philosophy of life:

There must be some, however, who still wonder what a little land like Norway can do for peace, freedom, and reason's sake in a world of unpeace, unfreedom, and unreason. We cannot accomplish anything by bullets and gunpowder. With weapons and national strength, a little nation fails miserably. . . . The task of the small nation is no longer in the fight, but rather in speaking to the conscience by its example. These are the spiritual weapons that we Norsemen may use in the fight for reason and international peace.

Likewise for a small national group like the Norse in Canada. We are poor and widely scattered. . . . It is impossible for the Norse folk-group as such to elect a crossing-sweeper, let alone a member of parliament. But we can work by our *quality*. Some things weigh more heavily in the scale than others do: that is assuredly according to the order of nature. But that leads one on to the supreme legacy of personality. A person—or, for that matter, a national group—without personality is the most miserable thing on God's green earth. (May 25, 1939)

Three Swedish-Canadian weeklies—*Canada-Tidningen* of Winnipeg, edited by Mr. Esse Ljungh, *Canada Posten* of Winnipeg, edited by Mr. F. O. Gustafson, and *Nya Svenska Pressen* of Vancouver, edited by Mr. M. M. Lindfords—can add little to the Norse statement of opinion; nor can Canada's one Danish paper, the weekly *Danske Herold* of Kentville, N.S., edited by Mr. Odin Kuntze. A strongly religious emphasis, chiefly Lutheran in background, is found in them all, and a repudiation of all political extremes, whether Fascist or Communist. The verdict of *Canada-Tidningen* is typical:

The ideology that is dominant just now in all Central Europe is a repudiation of all liberalism and of all human values. It is like a flood that washes away all the covering layers of civilization and sweeps against Christianity and the various Christian churches with like ruthlessness. (May 25, 1939)

The Icelandic-Canadians find expression through two weekly newspapers, *Lögberg* ("Law-Mountain", edited by

Einar Páll Jónsson) and *Heimskringla* ("The Globe", edited by Stefán Einarsson), both of Winnipeg. The main difference between these two papers is sectarian. *Lögberg* is strongly Lutheran in its church affiliations, while *Heimskringla* is closely associated with the Icelandic Unitarian church. Through close integration with Canadian life, the Icelandic-Canadians have become deeply interested in the question of Canada's national status. It was one of their leaders, Mr. Joseph Thorson, Federal member for Selkirk, who last session introduced a bill in the House of Commons seeking to define Canada's right to determine her own foreign policy in case of war. *Lögberg's* comment is one of approval:

> The gist of Mr. Thorson's bill has been urged more than once in the columns of this paper, namely that Canada should have full responsibility for the conduct of her own foreign policy, and that she should not be content that a government other than her own should be able to thrust her people inevitably into a war. (April 27, 1939)

And the editor goes on to quote, with evident satisfaction, Mr. Thorson's retort to an interpellation from Mr. Thomas L. Church, M.P., of Toronto:

> I was three years in the great World War, and served 18 months of that in the British Imperial Forces; and I can assure Mr. Church that a far greater proportion of my nationality volunteered for war service than did those of British stock in this country. Let no man imagine that I have not a full right to speak as a Canadian.

This concern over Canada's status does not imply unmitigated isolationism, but rather a grave disquiet, already widespread among Canadians of French and British origin, lest an Imperial cabinet should have power to plunge Canada into any and every war, regardless of Canadian opinion. That the Icelandic-Canadians are solidly opposed to the Nazi threat of today is borne out by an article by

Mr. W. J. Lindal, published in the issue of *Heimskringla* for April 5, 1939:

There is need for clarifying our attitude towards the present international situation. No one knows whither Hitler will turn next. . . . Canadians have asked themselves these same questions. There is only one answer—to show infallible unity, to stand together as one man!

Since the issues of the present war have become clearly crystallised, there has been resolute unanimity among the Canadian Scandinavians in supporting Canada against Hitler, not only with deep loyalty but with earnest determination.

(iv) JEWISH-CANADIAN OPINION

According to the last census, there were 156,726 Jews in Canada. Most of these represented pre-War immigration from Poland, Russia, and Rumania, plus natural increase. In this country, as elsewhere, they are almost entirely urban. Far from exemplifying, in accordance with Hitler's belief, a diabolic urge to mix with Aryan stock, less than one per cent. of these Jews have married Anglo-Canadian wives and less than one per cent. of the Jewesses have married Anglo-Canadian husbands. They are chiefly engaged in small retail businesses, in the fur trade, and in the cinema business. Of the latter two, they are coming to enjoy a comparative monopoly. Contrary again to Nazi theory, they have virtually no share in Canadian journalism, either financially or editorially, except in a few small papers, chiefly Yiddish, published by Jews for Jews.

As in Poland, from which the bulk of Canada's Jews derive, there are four main schools of Jewish political thought: (1) The Orthodox Group, consisting of classes that have kept their traditional faith and customs intact. They can be roughly divided into two sub-groups, the conservative party and a remaining non-political mass without self-conscious aims. (2) The Nationalist Group, who define the Jews as a nation and are predominantly secularist and Zionist in programme. Great stress is laid on support to Palestine or "Eretz Israel". (3) The Radical Group, tending in Canada to become completely Communist in principle. (4) The Assimilation Group, who deny in principle the existence of Jewish nationality and reduce it to a mere matter of confessional differentiation. This group tend more and more to regard themselves simply as "Canadians".

There are seven Jewish newspapers in Canada, viz: the daily *Kanader Adler* ("Canadian Eagle"), of Montreal; the daily *Juedischer Journal* ("Hebrew Journal"), of Toronto; the weekly *Der Kampf* ("The Struggle"), of Toronto; the semi-weekly *Israelite Press*, of Winnipeg; the weekly *Canadian Jewish Chronicle*, of Montreal; the weekly *Canadian Jewish Review*, of Montreal; and the weekly *Jewish Post*, of Winnipeg. The first four of these are printed in Yiddish and the last three in English.

Most of the foregoing (e.g. the *Israelite Press*) are simply good business enterprises and attempt to interest the highest common factor in all the Jewish groups rather than to advance the sectional programme of one group. Some papers, e.g. *The Canadian Jewish Chronicle* and the *Kanader Adler* lean towards the Nationalist (Zionist) cause, and were for a time highly critical of the recent British policy in Palestine. Realization soon came, however, of the difficulties faced by Britain in ensuring Arab loyalty as a show-down with Hitlerism grew imminent, and Canadian Jewry has been second to none in condemning Nazi Germany and in professing loyalty to Britain:

When, moreover, one considers the prevalence of those phobias and epidemics of hatred that sweep across certain lands, phenomena from which Britain is singularly free, one can readily understand the full import and significance of Jewish loyalty to the Crown. It is not mere lip-service; it is not simple acquiescent genuflection; it is not bare formal obeisance. It is rather the oath of allegiance triply sworn, the fidelity that cannot be broken, the loyalty that can neither be assailed nor assoiled. (*Canadian Jewish Chronicle*, May 12, 1939)

There has been a natural tendency to fear and oppose Nazi agents and their anti-Semitic propaganda in Canada:

We are certain that it is no secret for the Federal police what is occurring between the Hitler agents and their various organizations both here (Montreal) and in other parts of the country. The people in Western Canada have recently become enraged against the activity of the Nazis, and the Federal government would be complying with the wish of the majority of citizens in the Dominion if it would at last take some measures to make the Hitlerites feel that Canada is not Germany. (*Kanader Adler*, May 5, 1939)

One Jewish paper, *Der Kampf*, of Toronto, is openly Communist and has been vehement in enunciating the theory that a peace front against Hitler, organized by Soviet Russia, is the hope of the world, and that England and France have been traitors to civilization in not embracing a peace front on Stalin's terms:

But just as in the general occurrences during the last two decades there comes just from one corner of the world a brilliant light, the new, free spirit of the Soviet Union, thus similarly in the question of fighting the war-incendiarists, the Soviet Union is the only country from which there is coming an unrelenting struggle for a real alliance against the aggressors. The Soviet Union is the very backbone of peace in this world.

The Fascist aggressors and the murderous Japanese Imperialists can be stopped only by means of an alliance such as the Soviet Union demands. And when a quarter of a century since the last world war broke out is being observed now, it is necessary to strengthen the struggle so that the devilish play of the Chamberlains may be stopped and the democratic force against the aggressors may become hardened. (*Der Kampf*, June 30, 1939)

The conditions under which the present War has broken out and developed, have produced striking modifications in the foregoing attitudes. All references to the former bickering between Nationalists and Assimilationists, Hebraic conservatives and Yiddish secularists, Rightists and Leftists, have entirely disappeared. The sweep of the anti-Semitic Nazi avalanche over Poland, where most of their kindred live, together with the encouragement and cooperation that Hitler has received from Stalin, has brought to the Canadian Jews a unity of opinion and purpose that they have never known before. All are united in their condemnation of Germany, their appeal for Jewish enlistment to help England, and, even in the case of the Leftist paper, *Der Kampf*, their bitter denunciation of Soviet Russia. They are prepared to work, fight, and sacrifice to the utmost in order to prove their affectionate loyalty to Canada and to defeat the intolerant campaign of Nazidom in the world.

The anti-Semitism that has reared its head in parts of Canada in recent years they rightly ascribe, in the main, to Nazi activities. In extensive areas of English and French Canadian opinion, the Jew had not been popular, but aggressive intolerance had been alien to the Canadian spirit and tradition. That rattlesnake entered our Eden with the Nazi's penetrative campaign from 1933 on. Not only was the Nazi *Deutsche Zeitung fuer Canada* virulent in its attacks, in keeping with the motivation of the Deutsche Bund, the Deutsche Arbeitsfront, and the Canadian branch of the Nazi party. The Nazi-sponsored National Unity Party of Monsieur Adrien Arcand has also been active and has even outdone the Nazis in reviling the Jews and inciting Canadians to take action against them. Thousands of copies of that proven forgery, *The*

Protocols of the Elders of Zion, have been printed and circulated in Montreal and Toronto, as well as such false and
libellous works as *The Code of the Jews* and *The Key to the
Mystery.* The Italian weekly, *Il Bollettino Italo-Canadese,*
of Toronto, has also collaborated in these attacks on
Jewry; and many Ukrainian-Canadian fascists have joined
zealously in the hue and cry. Most of the Jew-baiting
organizations seem to have been influenced, directly or
indirectly, by the Nazis. At any rate, the standard Nazi
machinery of invasion (*viz.*: (1) mobilization of *Reichsdeutsche* and *Volksdeutsche,* and (2) the encouragement of
native fascist groups), has in Canada likewise betrayed
that odour of *Judenhass* that clings to all their works.

(v) POLISH-CANADIAN OPINION

Citizens of Polish extraction constitute the seventh largest national group in Canada. Of the 136,211 recorded in
1931, less than one-half were Canadian-born and over 85
per cent. belonged to the Roman Catholic church. Unlike the Ukrainians, they have developed neither Communist nor Fascist tendencies, and do not constitute a
militant element in Canadian life. Two main organizations
have tended to direct their cultural activities, *viz.*: (1) the
Associated Poles of Canada, a group of parish clubs,
largely organized and controlled by the Roman Catholic
church, and (2) the Federation of Polish Societies in
Canada, a more purely secular alignment of cultural and
athletic groups, of which the Sokol (or "Falcon") Gym-
nastic Association is a typical example. Winnipeg is the
main centre of their cultural life, and here are published
the only Polish newspapers in Canada, *viz.*: *Gazeta Katolicka* ("The Catholic Gazette", a weekly, edited by Mr.
Jan S. Pazdor), representing the Associated Poles, and

Czas ("The Times", a weekly, edited by Mr. W. A. Drelenkiewicz), which is the official organ of the Federation of Polish Societies in Canada.

Sympathy with Polish nationalism is a force uniting all Canadian Poles. Towards Hitler and the German threat against Danzig, the Corridor, and Polish independence, the attitude of the whole community is single and resolute:

> Facing the united front of the whole Polish nation, Hitler will perhaps try to change his plans, but he will not abandon his plans until he is compelled to do so by force.   (*Czas*, April 4, 1939)

> The Third Reich is a great Power. Napoleonic France was even greater, yet it was overcome, although its army was led by the greatest general in the world.   (*Czas*, February 21, 1939)

> A more ignoble end awaits Hitler than even that of the former Kaiser, for no country will be willing to accept him when his own country turns against his madness.   (*Czas*, April 11, 1939)

> In the heart and soul of Catholic Poles, the ideal of Poland is expressed in the traditional slogan of "free, united, independent, and Catholic".   (*Gazeta Katolicka*, January 4, 1939)

> We have never yet lost out in decisive issues with the German state. The unhealthy appetite of the "Herrenvolk", who, through their belief in the right of might, made pretensions to rule the world, was restrained in the first place by Poland. (*Gazeta Katolicka*, April 26, 1939)

With the heightening of the German threat during the past year, there has arisen in Canada the Polish Maritime League, headed by Dr. Frank Sedziak of Winnipeg, which seeks to emphasize the fact that the Corridor is racially and historically Polish and that the loss of Poland's Baltic ports would be fatal to her national existence. Even more eloquently expressive of the Canadian-Polish interest in the fate of the Motherland has been the forwarding of very large volunteer subscriptions of money to the Polish government, to assist it in its struggle against German aggression.

Both *Gazeta Katolicka* and *Czas* are hostile towards Soviet Russia. *Gazeta Katolicka* expresses freely that detestation of Communism which is everywhere felt by Roman Catholicism, while *Czas*, which in all its editorials approximates more closely to the point of view of the present Polish government, thinks rather in political terms and might be prepared to accept Russian backing to "stop Hitler", provided there were no occupation of Polish or Lithuanian territory by Soviet troops:

Soviet Russia, because of its criminal abuse of power, is now entering upon a stage of exhaustion. From December 1937 to December 1938, they killed 40,000 men who opposed the present régime, and they threw 500,000 others into prison. Meantime, they are torturing ten million persons, a fantastic figure, in their concentration camps. (*Gazeta Katolicka*, January 25, 1939)

Diplomatic circles are coming to the conclusion that Polish-Soviet relations are assuming such a form as is desired both in Paris and in London. (*Czas*, May 30, 1939)

While both Germany and Russia are hated and feared by all Poles, Italy, on the contrary, is the object of their affectionate good will. As in the case of French-Canadian Catholicism in Quebec, Polish-Canadian Catholicism has warm admiration for Catholic Italy:

The sympathy of the Italian people was well expressed by Mussolini, speaking to the Polish delegation of legionaries in December 1937, when he said: "You, gentlemen, have on several occasions had a chance to experience how the Italian nation sympathizes with the Poles." . . . The visit of Foreign Minister Ciano in Warsaw, being an answer to last year's visit of Foreign Minister Beck to Rome, shows the continuance of definite Polish-Italian collaboration. It is also a new manifestation of the age-old friendship between the two nations. (*Gazeta Katolicka*, May 15, 1939)

As the most prominent politicians point out, the document (the British guarantee to Poland) is a fatal blow to the aggressive ambition of Adolf Hitler, and also a painful blow to the Balkan ambitions of Benito Mussolini, whose messenger to Poland, Count

Galeazzo Ciano, failed to persuade Poland to join the Berlin-Rome Axis, in spite of the friendship between Poland and the great Italy of today.   (*Gazeta Katolicka*, April 12, 1939)

Good will is also freely expressed towards Hungary and Rumania.

With respect to the Ukrainian Question, the Polish-Canadians are, in their own way, as partisan as the Ukrainian-Canadians. They never weary in stressing the fact that it was the civil population of Lemberg, and not a Polish army, that drove the Ukrainian army out of that predominantly Polish city in November 1918; that the "pacification" of 1930 was in response to Ukrainian terrorism and assassination of the Irish Republican Army type; that Polish and Ukrainian populations are hopelessly intermarried and intermingled in Galicia; and that the Ukrainian Nationalists in Poland have never really wanted federal autonomy but rather an outright independence that would ride rough-shod over the predominantly Polish urban populations of the region. Naturally they have had no use for the Nazi suggestion that Poland's Ukrainians should be used as a lever to pry open the Soviet Ukraine for Western exploitation. The following quotations are typical:

There is no Ukrainian language, but only a Little Russian dialect. That is why it would be hard to build up an independent Ukrainian state capable of existing alone. (*Czas*, February 7, 1939)

Poland will not allow anyone else to solve her Ukrainian problem; for she wants to solve it herself. In their conference at Berchtesgaden, Col. Jozef Beck, Polish Minister of Foreign Affairs, told Chancellor Hitler very plainly, leaving no room for doubt, that Germany cannot reach the Ukraine in any other way than over the body of the last Polish soldier, or rather, of the last Pole. (*Gazeta Katolicka*, May 22, 1939)

Amid their bitter grief at the ruthless conquest of their country and their profound anxiety over the fate of their

kinfolk under Nazi or Soviet tyranny, they still show in-
domitable courage and hope in the future resurrection of
their murdered nation. "Jeszcze Polska nie zginela, póki
my zyjemy . . ." (Poland has not perished, as long as we
live . . .) is still the note of their old national anthem; and
they mingle their loyalty to Canada at war with their
agonized determination to help win freedom once again
through defeat of the Nazi system.

(vi) ITALIAN-CANADIAN OPINION

Canadian residents of Italian origin total approxi-
mately 100,000. Of these, in 1931, over 53 per cent. were
Canadian-born. Practically all the remainder had been
born in Italy, but two-thirds of these were naturalized
Canadians. Over 94 per cent. of the Italian-Canadians can
speak English or French; and over 93 per cent. belong to
the Roman Catholic Church. Their settlement has been
predominantly urban, and there are important "colonies"
in Montreal, Toronto, and Vancouver.

Two factors tend to influence their opinion on foreign
affairs: (1) their adherence to the Church of Rome, and
(2) the natural enthusiasm generated by the achievements
of the "New Italy". In keeping with the former, there are
intimate relationships with the Canadian French; and as
a result of the latter, there is proud jubilation over the
transformation which Signor Mussolini has brought about
in their homeland.

The chief Italian newspaper in Canada is a Montreal
weekly, formerly called simply *Italia* but more recently rechristened *L'Italia Nuova* ("The New Italy"). It is a
large, well-edited publication, with some fourteen pages in
Italian and single-page supplements in French and in
English. Smaller in format and almost identical in view-

point is the weekly *Il Bollettino Italo-Canadese* ("The Italian-Canadian Bulletin") of Toronto.

In many respects, the Canadian Italians hold opinions similar to those of the Canadian French. There is the same emphasis on loyalty to Canada (not the Empire or the Commonwealth), the same hatred of Communism, and the same dominant Catholicism. There were eloquent tributes to King George VI and Queen Elizabeth during the royal visit of 1939:

> On this happy occasion, we are happy to renew to the King and Queen the sentiments of loyalty and devotion of all Italian-Canadians, as well as that of all immigrants of Italian race, who have freely adopted British citizenship and who, in serving with all their strength and integrity the country of their choice, still bear in their hearts the Fatherland of their origin. . . .
>
> And as Mr. La Guardia—whom no one, to be sure, accused of being an agent of Fascist propaganda—added that these sentiments did not prevent him from being a loyal American, so we—most proud of our Italian origin—feel that we are not less "most loyal Canadians", devoted and respectful subjects of this fair Canada, which, modestly but surely, we have helped to make great by our toil.   (*L'Italia Nuova*, May 13, 1939)

An interesting apologia for the Italian-Canadians appears in *Il Bollettino Italo-Canadese* for May 2, 1939:

> In some Canadian circles, private and public, a hostile attitude towards Italy is taken, justifying itself by saying that Italy is a country hostile to Canada and to England. Without a doubt this impression has been created by the press campaign, which has reached fantastic proportions.
>
> Until proof to the contrary exists, there is between Italy and England the so-called "Gentleman's Agreement", which is valid likewise for the countries of the British Empire. Between Canada and Italy there has not been the slightest incident. The attitude of Italy towards Canada has been most respectful and towards England friendly. Why, therefore, create an artificial spirit of hostility, where no reason for any exists?
>
> To create in Canada an anti-Italian phenomenon, is not political wisdom in a country that has strong minorities of all races. The

Canadian minorities will always have reason to suspect the majority, and one will end by delaying still more the blending of the people, will emphasize yet more those divisions of race which they deprecate in other countries, and will finally create a problem of minorities comparable to those in Europe.

Do not imagine that Italy wants to make Fascist propaganda in order to transform Canada into a totalitarian state. That is the role of the Communists. Remember what Mussolini has said: "Fascism is not a commodity for export." The so-called Fascist Italian activities in Canada do not go beyond making Italy known a little, avoiding the mistakes that have worked to its harm, and maintaining the best relations between the two countries.

The only anti-Canadian activity of the citizens of Italian origin in Canada is that of the Communist group, with which the great majority of Italian-Canadians absolutely refuse to be identified. All the others are excellent citizens, inferior to those of no other race, and do not deserve to be made the objects of discrimination at this delicate moment.

Side by side with this it is interesting to place the following excerpt from an article entitled "England is not Christian":

The attitude of the Anglican Church is such that in 1931 it consented to birth control. In 1938, it showed clearly that it no longer had any clear distinction between a human being elevated to a supernatural order and the spirit that remains in a state of nature. This is Pelagianism, religious naturalism, Christianity without the supernatural. It is very difficult to see how England is Christian or how the English can have a Christian conscience. The leaders of the Church of England busy themselves more willingly with political problems than with religious ones; and in politics, where they are most powerful, they introduce that lack of Christianity which characterizes "perfidious Albion". (*Il Bollettino Italo-Canadese*, June 29, 1939)

The motivation of the foregoing may be religious rather than political. For downright political hostility, however, it would be hard to find anything more vituperative than the following article contributed by M. Thomas-Louis Bergeron to the French page of *L'Italia Nuova* for May

20, 1939—an article betraying not only an intriguing contempt for Hitler but also an old style Frenchman's implacable hatred for Britain:

Hitler is a very disagreeable specimen: dangerous for his neighbors, irritating to his rivals, harsh towards his enemies. He is a sort of accomplished corporal—surly, authoritarian, and violent. One must note, however, that one of his most irritating sides is precisely that in which he believes he must imitate the democracies: making a racket. This dictator is a man of plebiscites, of public harangues based on parliamentary declamations, a man of boastfulness, of the most astonishing accusations compounded of recklessness and lies. He wishes, like the parliamentarians, to let the masses believe that it is themselves who are governing, and that he is only the instrument of their will, the servant of their interests. For this, he must violate the truth, make fanatics, inspire hatred, stir up discord, sow terror, beat down resistance, and stifle opposition, as our parliamentarians do. . . .

It is not without reason that men accuse and distrust him. He did not invent his misdeeds. He found his precedents in history and only needed to glean a few. He has violated treaties? That is an old game. He can reply to England that if she has succeeded in re-establishing for herself an almost universal dictatorship, it is thanks to the policy of duplicity that she has practised for almost three centuries. To betray today's ally if he becomes too strong, to help the enemy of yesterday if he becomes too weak to assure for her the game of balance—that is the diplomacy of England, the diplomacy that has earned for her the title of "perfidious Albion". From 1920 to 1936, she abandoned France, whose prestige embarrassed her, and helped in the restoration of Germany. The German rearmament, the occupation of the Rhineland by German troops, the return of the Saar to Germany, the re-establishment of the German fleet—all this was done under the indulgent eye of London. But this scaffolding might collapse suddenly. Hitler might not be able to maintain his mastery of Germany. It was therefore necessary to oppose another power to France. Therefore London embroiled France and Italy by the imbecile device of economic sanctions, on the occasion of the Ethiopian adventure. . . .

If Europe is faced today with one of the greatest perils that ever threatened her, it is because of England's political trickery. And it is this same trickery that would have Canada ruin itself, men and means, in order to overthrow the powers that she set up—without wishing, I grant, to unite them at all—for the purpose of checking French power.

For centuries, a handful of islanders, in order to preserve their mastery of the world, have by treacherous and hypocritical policies sent people into atrocious butcheries in which they themselves engaged only in the shelter of foreign armies. The first to provoke conflicts but the last to enter the battle, they have always been the first to receive the fruits of victory under the wide-spread banner of democracy and liberty.

Finally, while the editors of these papers are scrupulous in avoiding any advocacy of Fascist policies in Canada, there is perhaps some significance in their reprinting of tendencious articles from *The Thunderbolt*, monthly publication of the Canadian Union of Fascists, the Anglo-Canadian branch of the Mosley organization in England, which is far more outspoken than any Italian-Canadian group. An English article in point is one written by Andrew Glen, urging the establishment in Canada of the "Corporate State", and reprinted in *Il Bollettino Italo-Canadese* for May 18, 1939:

A party government, of course, is not representative of the country; but a government consisting of representatives of the various occupational interests in Canada, each one elected by its own thoroughly organized group, could truly and rationally execute the Nation's business with a minimum of friction. A lawyer would not speak for agriculture, nor would a railwayman or a building trades' appointee be expected to deal with matters of finance. The talking, the squabbling, would be done within the respective groups, and the recommendations for the efficient and satisfactory operation of the industry or service passed upwards through regional committees for ratification by the supreme council, if they did not conflict with the general national plan and policy.   Our government would then be a group of administrators of the various departments of the Nation's life—a Board of Directors for the successful organization and management of the firm of The Dominion of Canada Unlimited.

Such a State presupposes the elimination of the class-war. Such a State demands of all members of the body corporate that they consider themselves not primarily manufacturers or farmers or doctors; not miners or teachers or engineers or housekeepers; but as Canadians. Ideological differences, partisan conflicts and personal gain would be melted into an intense patriotism. No organ or member of the human body can be neglected or in pain without causing injury and discomfort to the entire organism. All are one, one is all. That alone is the principle on which we can establish unity.

Is it too radical and fantastic? Other nations have achieved this spirit of unity. We may not like dictatorships, but the list is growing. France is the latest to be added. A strong movement is on foot in Britain to appoint a Comptroller for every industry. Plans for the mobilization of industry are said to have been prepared by the United States government for speedy adoption. But this is not necessarily a plea for unity for the vigorous prosecution of war. It is the demand of the twentieth century for the social organization of any civilized state.

Since the outbreak of the present war, the Italian-Canadian press has been loud in urging neutrality and such peace as was sought by the eleventh hour negotiations of Mussolini. Thus *Il Bollettino* for September 7th explains:

Italy's declaration of neutrality places Italians and Italian-Canadians in a delicate position, of which the people of our race take cognisance with a sense of responsibility that does honour to that worth of the Italian people which they do not belie in this critical moment. The Italians know what are their duties towards the country of which they are the guests. Those who have taken out Canadian citizenship know likewise what are the duties of the allegiance that they have assumed.

L'Italia Nuova for September 9th goes on to say:

For all these reasons, while bowing to all the decisions that the Federal Parliament of Ottawa—the supreme authority of that Canada in which we live and of which we are citizens—has taken, we yet express our wish and hope that the noble and generous efforts exerted by Mussolini for peace, in spite of the outbreak of hostilities, may succeed in giving favourable results. And let us express our sincere and profound confidence that He can succeed in this great and humane enterprise. When that has been said, let us cry with all our hearts: Long live Canada! Long live Italian-Canadian friendship, which no cloud ought to obscure! . . . The sagacious, honest, and loyal effort of Il Duce for the preservation of peace is the object of our greatest admiration and causes us once more to give thanks to Divine Providence for having presented Italy with the gift of this superior, unique, enlightened and infallible man.

There are marked evidences, however, especially since the aftermath of the Russo-German pact has brought about a Soviet occupation of Eastern Poland and placed the Balkans deeply in the shadow of Stalin's atheist legions, that this hesitant attitude of the Italian-Canadian press (too suggestive of a Duplessis infection) is not typical of the rank and file of the Canadian Italians, especially those who have been born in Canada. More representative of these is a recent news item in the Winnipeg *Evening Tribune*:

Young Canadians of Italian descent, gathered Tuesday night (October 3rd) at Holy Rosary (Italian) church, pledged full loyalty to Canada and declared their willingness to "defend in whatever way we can the liberties and democratic institutions of the British Commonwealth of Nations". The toast to King George VI was proposed by Pietro Colbertaldo, regent of the Italian vice-consulate. The regent also toasted Victor Emmanuele, King of Italy and Emperor of Ethiopia. Florence March, president of the Children of Mary Sodality of the parish, stated that though they revered the traditions and culture of their old homeland, Canadians of Italian origin look first to Canada. A resolution of loyalty was unanimously approved, to be forwarded to the Dominion Government.

(vii) RUSSIAN-CANADIAN OPINION

The Revised 1931 census figure for Canadians of Russian origin is 60,302. Of these, about two-thirds belong to the Doukhobor sect, which is non-political and non-combatant in orientation. Among the remainder the main organization is the Russian Workers' and Farmers' Association ("R.R.F.K."), which is Communist in trend.

The only Russian newspaper in Canada is the Communist tri-weekly, *Kanadsky Gudok* ("The Canadian Fiddle"), published in Winnipeg. Its editor, Mr. M. Yasny, is a gifted Jew, with a fine Russian style; and the enterprise seems to be largely Jewish in management.

The phraseology of "democracy" is incessantly employed, and the term is as constantly equated with "the great and happy Soviet Union". For the government of Great Britain, no terms of condemnation were, for a time, apparently too strong:

No government in the history of mankind was ever so contemptible in its methods or stooped so low in its wish to mislead the public as the present government of England.   (May 11, 1939)

Fear for the interests of his social class makes Chamberlain do things of unprecedented meanness. His political agents have begun to spread rumours that Poland and Rumania are against the conclusion of an Anglo-Soviet military alliance.   (May 11, 1939)

V. Molotov, President of the Council of the People's Commissars of the U.S.S.R., in his report on the foreign affairs of the U.S.S.R., gave a definite and unequivocal answer to the Munichites of the Anglo-French camp, saying that the Soviet nation has not forgotten their former deeds and has no reason to hope that they have changed now.   (June 3, 1939)

Kanadsky Gudok had similar denunciation for the present government of Canada:

On the First of May, the labour masses of Canada should firmly demand of Mackenzie King's government to change its foreign policy so that it may serve the interests of peace and not those of war. The Canadian government goes blindly on in the footsteps of Chamberlain's policy and thus shields Fascist aggression no less than the European Munichites.   (April 29, 1939)

Nevertheless the Minister of Justice (Mr. Lapointe) says that the Communists as much as the Fascists aim at the destruction of the democratic system. Mr. Heaps protested against this statement. By his words, Mr. Lapointe really prepares the way in Canada for that Fascism from which he pretends that he wishes to save it. (June 1, 1939)

In common with other Communist papers in Canada, it insisted on the theory that the English, the French, and the Poles actually sought to assist Hitler in his projected attack on the U.S.S.R.:

> During the past year, we witnessed the annexation of Czechoslovakia by the Hitlerites, of Albania by the Italians, and of Spain by the Italian-German interventionists. They succeeded in doing this through the help given them by the reactionary classes of England and France, who want to strengthen the Fascist countries and direct them against the Socialist Country. (April 29, 1939)
>
> It is more important to Beck to support Fascism than any national "honour". While speaking of the national "honour" of Poland, he is really more concerned with saving Hitler's "honour". (May 9, 1939)

The editorials of *Kanadsky Gudok* also stressed from time to time the necessity of purging the ranks of Russian-Canadian Communism of all elements that were not thoroughly reliable Stalinites:

> The more consolidated the ranks of the labour movement are, and the more united the Russian Workers' and Farmers' Association in Canada is, the more easily we can realize our task of winning over the whole of the Russian colony in Canada to the side of the democratic movement. This fact dictates to us that it is necessary to keep the ranks of the R.R.F.K. clean, not to admit any treacherous elements into the association, and to weed out all such elements from the progressive associations. (May 20, 1939)

One's general impression of Canada's Russians, therefore, was that of an active, astute, and well-disciplined Communist party.

The sudden, amazing announcement of a Nazi-Soviet pact, followed by the partition of Poland, has been a startling blow to this group. The *Kanadsky Gudok* categorically supported Canada in its war effort, and in an article of September 9th, threw some light on the position of the Doukhobors:

World democracy is endangered. German fascism is on the aggressive. Its aims are to destroy democracy in Europe and throughout the whole world. That is why all progressive people support the countries that are taking action on the side of Poland. That is why they want to see Canada play an honourable rôle in this conflict. Something we cannot deny is that our entire Russian youth is for destroying fascism. The Russian youth, and particularly the Doukhobors, although the latter may not be active and direct participants in the front lines, will show their sympathies and will be definitely on the side of democracy, morally supporting the democratic peace front.

The subsequent action of the Russian army in occupying Eastern Poland has, however, evoked so significant a response that knowledge of it is important to all Canadians. *Kanadsky Gudok* for October 14th has the following explanation to give:

Entry of the Soviet Union's Red Army into what had formerly been Poland, on September 17th of this year, gave those people working in the interests of reaction in Canada an abundance of material for their slanderous propaganda against the Soviet Union. "Hitler and Stalin Partition Poland", "Poland Destroyed by Reds and Nazis", read the headlines. Columnists and reporters wrote article after article lamenting the fate of Poland and condemning the Soviet government for ordering its troops across the border.

According to all the stuff that has been printed in the daily newspapers since that date, one would be led to believe that the Soviet Union is to blame for all that took place in Poland and *that the war is being fought against the Soviet Union and not against Germany*. The reports have tried to bring out that the Red Army and the army of Hitler pursue one and the same policy. In their desperate attempt to conceal the real truth they say that the aggression policy of Fascist Germany and the Soviet Union's policy of international peace are one and the same policy.

But is all this true? Are the Red Army and the army of Fascist Germany the same? Do they pursue the same policy? Is the Red Army an army of aggression?

There can be only one answer to all these questions: NO!

It is very profitable for the capitalist classes here in Canada to keep the people in ignorance of all that is taking place. They therefore pay those with high literary ability to distort facts and present them in the form most suitable to them.

The objectives of these two armies, representing two distinctly different trends, are as far apart as the two shores of the Atlantic. Their interests are irreconcilable.

Hitler fascism, inspired and supported by the international financiers in the face of the Munich men, invaded the territories of Poland with the objective of placing it under fascist dictatorship. The "umbrella boys" wanted Hitler to strengthen his base to carry out the ultimate objective: to wage a war against the Soviet Union, a country that has liberated itself from the grip of the capitalist bondholders.

Hitler's plan was to occupy Poland, force his way through Rumania to the Black Sea, a very strategic location for an attack against the Soviet Union. But thanks to the timely actions of the Soviet government the execution of this plan fell through.

The Red Army did not cross the frontiers the same way that Hitler's fascist army did. It was only after Colonel Beck, Count Raczinski, and the other members of the Polish government betrayed their country and were in exile, leaving the Polish people, still resisting fascist aggression, to their fate, that the Soviet troops entered the country. Their drive was to cut off the fascist armies from the Rumanian frontier, and they succeeded in their undertaking, thus eliminating the danger of Hitler forcing his way to the Black Sea.

The people of Polish White Russia and the Polish Ukraine, territories occupied by the Red Army, welcome it. They realize in the Red Army the force that will do away with the exploitation of the poor people by the rich in that territory for ever and ever. The people of the Soviet Union hail their government for defending the population of Polish White Russia and the Polish Ukraine, blood-brothers of the people of Soviet White Russia and the Soviet Ukraine, for saving them from falling under the rule of fascism, and for safeguarding the interests of the U.S.S.R.

Regardless of how much our dailies write on the present situation, regardless of how much they distort facts, the people know for themselves the difference between oppression and liberty; they know for themselves that the interests of the Soviet Government are the interests of the entire working class of the world. History will prove that the actions of the Soviet Government and of the Red Army in the present swiftly changing situation are just and timely.

(viii) FINNISH-CANADIAN OPINION

The Finnish language belongs to the Turanian family, with Estonian and Magyar as its nearest European cousins. Swedish blood and culture, however, have entered very extensively into the making of the modern nation, and it is common for the Finns, who are predominantly Lutheran, to refer to their country as "Scandinavian". As a member of the "Oslo Group", Finland is intimately related to Sweden, Denmark and Norway, both in policy and in civilization.

The Finns in Canada numbered 21,494 in 1921, and by 1931 had more than doubled, through immigration, to a total of 43,885, of whom 1,778 were Swedish-speaking. Prominent among the post-war immigrants were members of the defeated Communist army in Finland, which had almost succeeded in 1919 in adding their country to the Soviet Union. As a result, the most active element among the Finno-Canadians is Communist in politics, giving rise to the impression that all Canadian Finns are Communists. This is far from being the case, for of the three Finnish newspapers in Canada only one, the daily *Vapaus* ("Liberty") of Sudbury, is definitely Moscophil in opinion. The other two are the weekly *Vapaa Sana* ("Free Press") of Toronto, which is a bourgeois, anti-Communist paper, plentifully sprinkled with Lutheran and Baptist church news, and the weekly *Canadan Uutiset* ("The Canadian News") of Port Arthur, which is mildly Socialist but not Communist.

Vapaa Sana comes perhaps closest to the predominant opinion of Finland today. Its attitude towards Hitler and a Central European alignment is made clear in an editorial of May 10th:

Germany surprised the world last week by making an offer to the four Scandinavian countries to sign a non-aggression pact. This offer is remarkable because a non-aggression pact with the Scandinavian countries is without any military significance whatever.

The four Nordic countries, Finland, Sweden, Norway and Denmark, have in recent years maintained a policy of keeping clear from the big nations and refusing to sign any agreements with the World Powers. This policy has recently been implemented in such a fashion that all the Nordic countries have made common cause, and each country has agreed not to sign any pacts without discussing it with the others.

The best explanation of this neutrality policy has been given by Mr. Humbro, the Speaker of the Norwegian parliament, viz.: that in the case of a world war there will need to be at least one place where the world's present civilization can survive, and that place is Scandinavia.

Scandinavia does not want to get mixed up with other nations' affairs, and hopes that nobody will meddle in Scandinavian affairs. We must therefore wait and see what is to be the result of Hitler's new venture, the only aim of which is to get Finland, Sweden, Norway, and Denmark to surrender their neutral standing.

On the other hand, their attitude towards Communism is clearly antagonistic:

The Central Committee of the Finnish Communistic societies in Canada recently held a meeting in Port Arthur. It is a matter on which we wish to express ourselves, especially since things were discussed at that meeting that concern us other Finlanders in Canada. According to the Communist newspaper *Vapaus*, they discussed the advisability of linking up the Finnish Communist Party in Canada with the existing workers' associations in Finland. The result was that they decided to affiliate with the Social Democratic Party of Finland.

But we, who do not approve of politics of this sort, will consider it our duty to point out to Finnish immigrants in this country what kind of treacherous ways the Finnish Communists use in order to win them over to their party by false promises and wrong impressions.

They will not be able to go through with their scheme, however, for the Social Democratic Party of Finland cannot be duped. It knows quite well that the Communists here do not represent the entire Finnish population in Canada, and therefore they will receive a very cold reception.

This paper of ours, which appears in thousands of Canadian-Finnish homes, will once in a while unmask the Communists when they are trying to perpetrate some of their schemes. (June 3, 1939)

Not many years ago, the Communists called Finland a land of oppression and capitalism; and today they want to unite with the Finnish Social Democratic Party under the same flag! All this is an insult to the Finnish flag. (May 13, 1939)

Canadan Uutiset is published in a very radical community, but its opinions seem to follow a moderate middle course, seeking strategically a highest common factor amongst its possible subscribers. The following editorial of May 3, 1939, is typical:

Rulers have always existed in the world who have thrown sand in the eyes of the people, in order that they may not see the misery, distress, and poverty in their own country. One of the most recent examples of throwing sand in the people's eyes was given by Mussolini, in a speech at Rome, when he shouted: "We consider eternal peace as being the foundation of civilization!"

Let us look around, at Finland for example, and we shall easily discover that during the last peaceful decennium it has made unbelievable progress in education, because its development has taken place without any political disturbance. But if it had been necessary to use this dynamic for making progress in the art of war, in national defence, or in campaigns of annexation, then all that has now been achieved would exist only as shadows, or scarcely even that.

On the other hand, the achievements of democratic countries cannot be considered ideal, for the most part because there is such antagonism between the different political parties that the government has not been able to mobilize all its ability and energy for united action. We all know what difficulty the people of Canada and the United States have had on account of unemployment. It is no secret that different parties and individuals have impeded reforms by first looking out for themselves and their own interests. We know that in Canada, for example, mismanagement exists, caused by selfish persons, and that this has caused the people to lose some of their rights, and that this has not been reformed or changed.

These faults of democracy cannot be cured by dictatorship. In order that democracy may be what it should be, we ourselves must all be transformed. Let us use the following saying as a motto: The good of our country comes before party differences.

It is in *Vapaus*, of Sudbury, that the Communist point of view becomes explicit. The ideal conditions prevailing in the U.S.S.R. are a matter of constant emphasis, as in the following editorial note:

Teachers are rewarded in Soviet Russia. The leaders of the Central Committee of Soviet Russia have just rewarded with decorations over 4,000 specially worthy country school-teachers. Of these, 400 received the highest decoration of Soviet Russia, the Order of Lenin. This shows the high esteem of the U.S.S.R. for patriotism and for teaching, in support of which large sums of money are spent every year. (May 15, 1939)

Under the heading, "The Fascist Propaganda of the Big Proprietors", it writes on May 27th:

Roger W. Babson is a propagandist, who reveals more openly than other writers of the moneyed aristocracy the future plans of the big proprietors. In his latest article, he mentions again that the workers receive too much pay and that the proprietors are the "forgotten men". "Nobody," he continues, "likes the systems of Germany, Italy, and Japan, but at least they get something done. We need to return to the days of free trade and an unrestricted labour market."

Its position with regard to foreign policies is indicated in an editorial note of May 13th:

The French Communist deputy, Gabriel Peri, spoke Thursday in the Chamber of Deputies in favour of collective policies and against any appeasement of the aggressors. We shall have to stop giving in to the aggressors and continuing in the spirit of the Munich agreement. We must let the Fascist dictators understand that times have changed, and that there will be no more flying visits to Berchtesgaden, Munich, or the Vatican.

The Moscow newspaper, *Izvestia*, condemns the ways of Chamberlain and Daladier, ways that must be changed if we are to prevent war. The people of Canada are also affected by this crisis, for in case of war we shall have to pay dearly. We ought therefore to demand a world conference of all existing workers' organizations. During such a conference, we can, and also will, decide on united policies with respect to political questions of world-wide importance.

In domestic politics, *Vapaus* strongly supports the "New Democracy" movement of Mr. W. D. Herridge, and urges all Communists to take an active part in it.

In war-time, however, all these opinions are overshadowed by the single resolution to support Canada.

(ix) HUNGARIAN-CANADIAN OPINION

The census of 1921 showed only 13,181 Hungarians in Canada. By the census of 1931, this figure had been trebled to 40,582. The heavy post-war immigration was mainly of two sorts: (1) Magyar-speaking refugees from the extensive provinces (nearly three-quarters of historic Hungary) that had been turned over to the tender mercies of Jugoslavia, Rumania, and Czechoslovakia, and (2) Communist fugitives, often Jewish, who had taken part in the brief but bloody régime of Béla Kún. These two groups have produced in Canada two violently antagonistic schools of Hungarian opinion—the one, nationalist and revisionist, the other, Communist and revolutionary.

The former school is expressed journalistically by the semi-weekly *Kanadai Magyar Ujság* ("Canadian Hungarian News") of Winnipeg, edited by Mr. Gusztav Nemes. It represents the great bulk of Canada's Hungarians, both Catholic and Protestant, and stands for a diligent and law-abiding Canadianism. So far as this group is concerned, its clubs are almost entirely parish

societies under the aegis of the Church. They have no
Hungarian-Canadian organizations that are militant or
Fascist in character. In sentiment, they are strongly anti-
Communist and equally fervent in their love of historic
Hungary and their desire for the righting of the injustices
of Trianon. They repudiate the Hungarian Communists of
Canada as being traitors to Hungary and to the Magyar
character:

We declare that a true Magyar can never be a revolutionary, an
anarchist. A Magyar is always a law-abiding, peaceful, diligent and
industrious citizen in every country, even as he is here in Canada;
for this we claim and profess among our Canadian hosts also.
(April 7, 1939)

How long will Canadians tolerate the abuse of the Communists?
How long will they permit this group of a few persons, in the name
of our respected Magyar community in Canada, to befoul our names
and the efforts of the disciples of pure truth? . . . And finally, how
long will they permit these vulgar ruffians to accuse Chamberlain,
Horthy, and Mackenzie King of treason? They who see only in the
mass-murderer Stalin the embodiment of morality and the height
of purity? To whom the Magyar tongue's only use is to defame
their old country and their new one? (April 28, 1939)

Hitler is rarely mentioned, for the Magyars do not like the
Germans and such unwilling co-operation as is now given
by the Hungarian government is given under duress.
Towards Italy, on the other hand, there is a spirit of warm
friendship, due not only to the dominant Catholicism of
both countries but also to the consistent sympathy that
Italy has shown for the sufferings of Hungary. In ideology,
however, neither Fascism nor Naziism has had any great
appeal to most Hungarians. Towards the Czech and the
Rumanian, they feel revengeful hatred, and for the Serb a
dislike that is tempered with admiration for his quality as
a soldier. They are warm in their friendship for the Poles,
and intense in their fear of the Russians.

So far as Canadian foreign policy is concerned, it is their devout hope that Canada may not be involved in any European war in which their new loyalty to Canada would be in conflict with their old affection for Hungary; and if such a tragic struggle should come, they trust that they will never be asked to engage in actual fighting against the troops of their ancient Homeland. An editorial of March 31, 1939, sets this attitude forth in considerable detail:

For weeks past, words have been ringing in the parliaments of the provinces and the Dominion as to what will be the standpoint of Canada in the case of a possible European war. In these battles of words there is reflected that news-propaganda which irresponsibly stirs up souls with furious bloodthirsty patriotism. But on the other side again voices are heard that permit one to infer that in this country there are in large numbers those as well who are not willing to sacrifice for foreign interests their bodily health, their souls' integrity, the happiness of family life, and perhaps their lives as well. . . . In the two neighbouring eastern provinces, there are two opposed views. The one is the French-Canadian, the other expresses itself in the English tradition of political service. Canada, since it forms an organic part of the English world-empire, has for long decades past drawn from the Motherland, and still draws today, immeasurable economic and moral values. Canada developed in the shelter of this democratic world-power, as it still does. If her population, native-born or immigrant, expects from England the economic and above all the moral support that England in turn expects from Canada, it will be speedily given when a crisis demands it. This is an important consideration, and we understand that it is a proper one. To us Magyar-Canadians, who have sworn loyalty to this country, there is equally a moral obligation to offer our services for it, if the majority of the country so decides. Thence, however, we can rest assured that whatever forms enmity and hatred may take in the case of a possible European war, they will not force us to bear arms against our land of birth and to fight against its interests. Every Canadian leader, however, expects unconditionally that we shall be loyal citizens in this country, which offers a livelihood, repose, and above all freedom to every man, regardless of what country he was a citizen in former times.

The royal visit of May 1939 evoked the following comment:

There can be no doubt that in the course of the royal visit the royal couple, by their charming manners and their gracious mingling and conversing with the masses have softened and kindled all hearts, making the English friendship more glorious and appealing also to the emotions of the French-Canadians. The King and Queen have stolen their way into the heart of Canada, and thus we too, the Magyars of Canada, welcome them! (May 26, 1939)

The Communist minority among the Hungarian-Canadians is represented by the tri-weekly *Kanadai Magyar Munkás* ("Canadian Hungarian Worker"), edited anonymously in Toronto. Its tone and policy are indistinguishable from those of the other vernacular Communist newspapers in Canada. "Democracy" is the ever-present and sacred word, and the governments of Canada, Britain, and Hungary were long denounced as Fascist, reactionary, and betrayers of humanity. Typical of the style of the *Kanadai Magyar Munkás* are the following resolutions, passed on June 4, 1939, by those present at the newspaper's annual picnic, and later printed in the issue of June 10th and forwarded to the Prime Minister as the opinion of the true Hungarian citizens of Canada:

1. *In foreign policy:*

(a) In the most thorough-going way they condemn the foreign policy of the Hungarian government in support of Hitler and Mussolini, by which they not only imperil Hungarian independence to the uttermost but also help to support the Fascist powers in threatening the independence of other nations and endanger us all with a world war.

(b) They desire to support Canadian democracy, so that through British democracy and every other possible way they know of they may protect their own security and help to create a world peace-front against the continuance and extension of Fascism.

2. In domestic policy:

(a) In the most thorough-going way they condemn those little Magyar-Canadian papers, groups, and individuals who are making propaganda for the Fascist Hungarian government, and are recruiting partisans who not only injure the good name of Hungarians in Canada but thus help to undermine Canadian democracy and security, even as the German, Italian, and other Canadian Fascists are doing.

(b) They desire to support all institutions, groups, and individuals who, by disclosing and punishing the enemies of Canadian democracy and by the cultural, economic, and political extension and strengthening of democracy, work for Canadian security and the cause of peace.

More illustrative, however, of the real orientation of the *Kanadai Magyar Munkás* is the following excerpt from a display editorial in the issue of June 3, 1939:

A rich prize, to those who truly desire peace and are seeking the most effective measures for retaining it, was the speech of the People's Commissar for Foreign Affairs, Viaceszlav Molotov, with which, on the First of May, he spoke in the name of the 170,000,-000 people of the U.S.S.R. The world's peace-loving peoples waited with great anticipation for the speech of Molotov, for with the Fascist assaults and the treacheries of Munich in view, they are learning that the Homeland of Socialism truly upholds humanity in peace and progress.

The outbreak of war brought from the Hungarian nationalists of the *Kanadai Magyar Ujság* a categorical reiteration of their loyalty:

From the point of view of the Canadian Hungarian, only one aim, one fulfilment of duty, stands before us in these critical days: in spite of anxious interest in the land of our birth, we are unflinchingly loyal to the country of our adoption.   (September 8, 1939)

The Hungarian Communists, however, were caught off bases by the tempo of such events as the Russo-German pact, and continued their vilification of Chamberlain until the councils of the Communist Party in Canada finally set them right "in defence of Canada and democracy".

(x) JUGOSLAV-CANADIAN OPINION

The Canadian census of 1931 showed only 9,432 whose mother-tongue was Serb, Croat, or Slovene. No attempt was made to break this figure down further, but the fact that of these three groups in Canada only the Croats possess a vernacular newspaper seems to imply that they are by far the largest group. Over three-quarters of them entered Canada during the decade 1921-31, driven here by the repressive rule of the Serb majority; and they have naturally brought with them the intense political consciousness of the Croats in Europe. With the exception of a small but vigorous Communist minority, virtually all of the Croats in Canada identify themselves with the Croatian Peasant Party. They are anti-Serb, anti-Communist, and anti-Fascist, and have been vehement in their demands for Croatian autonomy within Jugoslavia on a democratic federal basis. Their chief organization in Canada is the H.B.Z. (Hrvatske Bratske Zajednice, "Croatian Brotherhood Association"), and their one newspaper is the weekly *Hrvatski Glas* ("The Croatian Voice") of Winnipeg, edited by Mr. Petar Stankovic.

This paper's open support of Dr. Machek's Peasant Party is shown, for example, by an editorial of February 15, 1939:

Reports from Belgrade say that Dr. Machek, the leader of the Croatian people, is the one who has the situation under his control. Long live our brave leader, Dr. Vladko Machek! Croatia must be free!

Speaking of Hitler's unsuccessful overtures to the Croats last spring, it says:

When Dr. Machek refused to be persuaded, Hitler then turned to the Serbs and promised them his help against the Croats. (May 23, 1939)

And then it adds:

Stojadinovich, with the connivance of the Serb Prince Paul, has entered into friendship with the two arch-devils of Europe, Hitler and Mussolini.

Its hostility to Communist activities within the Croat ranks in Canada is also clear:

Away with the Communist propaganda from the ranks of the H.B.Z.! The Communists have created divisions in our Association; but let us not be divided! Let us all be united as Croats! (April 18, 1939)

With the outbreak of war, the Croats, exultant over the recent agreement reached in Jugoslavia, whereby the Croats and Serbs at last present a united democratic front against German aggression, go on to express their loyalty to Canada:

The duty of every Canadian Croat, while rejoicing in the good fortune of his Motherland, is to give unqualified allegiance to Canada, the land of his adoption, and help those in authority in whatever capacity and in every way he can. The civilization of the world and the civilization of its people is worth striving for at this troubled hour, yes and worth fighting for unless we are prepared to spend our days under the tyrant's heel. (*Hrvatska Glas*, September 5, 1939)

(xi) OTHER EUROPEAN-CANADIAN GROUPS

There are still other Canadian groups of European origin, but these have no vernacular press in Canada, either because of the paucity of their numbers or because of the advanced degree of their assimilation to Canadian life.

Of these, the largest single group is the Dutch, totalling 148,962, the sixth largest national element in the Dominion. Apart from a monthly sheet of personals, entitled *Hollandia* and published in Chatham, Ontario, the Dutch-Canadians have no press. Virtually all are English-speaking; while 47 per cent. of their men and 44 per cent.

of their women are married to non-Dutch husbands. Fewer than 7 per cent. of them were born in the Netherlands, and nearly all the rest are Canadian-born and indistinguishable from our Anglo-Canadian population.

The last census showed 30,401 Czechs and Slovaks, but did not subdivide these two distinct groups further. Until last spring there was a Czech weekly paper, *Česke Noviny* ("The Czech News"), published in Montreal, but it gave up the ghost about the time that Germany seized Bohemia, apparently expiring as a result of the withdrawal of financial support through the Czech consulate-general. Czech opinion, as might be anticipated, was strongly anti-German, anti-Hungarian, and anti-Polish, and stressed the essentially democratic character of the Czech state. The Slovaks had no separate press, but there were many Canadian members of the Slovak League of America, which claims a membership of 300,000 and is bitterly anti-Czech and anti-Benesh.

There is likewise no Canadian press to represent our 29,056 Rumanians, 27,585 Belgians, 9,444 Greeks, 5,876 Lithuanians, 3,160 Bulgarians, and sundry Latvians, Estonians, Laplanders, Albanians, Swiss, Portuguese, and Spaniards. It is therefore very difficult to gauge the opinion of these small groups. A recent letter from a Lithuanian, published in the *Alberta Herold* (Nazi German), urged that the Germans should seize Danzig without delay and help the Lithuanians to seize Vilna. This may be only the attitude of an individual, but is more likely to be a typical Lithuanian-Canadian echo of the intransigent bitterness of the European Lithuanians against the Poles. On the other hand, the fact that the Poles in Canada have intermarried extensively and amicably with the Lithuanians (as also with the

Ukrainians) should prevent one from pushing a political
issue too far.

*   *   *   *   *   *

From the foregoing seventy pages there thus emerges a
most variegated mosaic of European-Canadian opinion,
which shapes itself nevertheless into a pattern of quite
astonishing unanimity on the issue of supporting Canada
in its armed opposition to Hitlerian aggression. The great
majority of our Germans are loyal Canadians. The conscious nationalists among our Ukrainians, Poles, Czechs,
Croats, and Magyars have no sympathy today with Nazi
expansion. Even some of our Communists of foreign stock
tend to condemn not only the violence of Hitler but the
predatory nationalism of Stalin. British and French
Canadians have demonstrated their sense of our national
unity; and now our two and a half million European-
Canadians give heartening assurance of their loyalty to
the Canadian nation. Canada is more united than ever
before in her history.

CHAPTER XII

A POLICY FOR CANADA

A N INTELLIGENT foreign policy for Canada in the present crisis is of the gravest importance. If we are to avoid disaster, both at home and abroad, we must carefully keep our intellectual balance, for "to think with one's blood" is to reduce oneself to the level of the beasts that perish, and that at a time when complex and fundamental issues are at stake.

It is perhaps axiomatic that the first and greatest principle of any Canadian foreign policy is the national interest of Canada itself; yet we shall need to keep the nature of that interest clearly before us. The majority of our citizens (whether Anglo-Canadians, French-Canadians, or European-Canadians) realize today that we are the objects of an evil and inexorable attack, against which we must defend ourselves and our civilization. In spite of the obfuscating influences of the American radio, the propaganda of Nazi organizations, and the parish dust and tumult of some provincial politicians, the bulk of our population sees Naziism as a tyrannic and intrusive force that will not suffer Canada or any other country to live at peace in religious, racial, and political liberty. Its propaganda has already insinuated itself into our national life and the anti-Semitic virus of race-hatred has been injected into our veins. Not only have the Reichsdeutsche in Canada been subjected to severe mobilizing pressure from abroad, and every Canadian of German origin been wooed by the alleged cultural agencies of the Reich, but our more violent and irresponsible elements, both French and British, have been encouraged in the formation of "blue-shirt" and "black-shirt" private armies on the familiar *Sturm-Abteilung* or *Schutz Staffel* model, in order to take over power in Canada by those methods of force and terror to which Hitler owes his dictatorship. That they prepare for such revolutionary action in the name of patriotism proves nothing except their shameless effrontery. Naziism, like Communism, is a dynamic force that is world-wide in its activities, and no one who has ever caught the perspective of its "global" ambitions can forget for a moment the fate that awaits human liberties everywhere if the Brown Terror should ultimately prevail. The *national interest* of Canada surely includes the defeat of that revolutionary force which seeks to impose its brutal mastery, directly or indirectly, on all countries, including our own. It is we who have been attacked.

A clear realization of this point will tend to give a unity of national purpose which is likewise essential to Canada's national interest. This is in no sense a British "imperial" war. It is true that the liberties of Britain and France, like those of all other European peoples, are threatened by the Nazi régime, and that the British are fighting for the survival of their own freedom; but the principle of national and personal liberty for all (including ourselves) is inextricably bound up with the victory or defeat of the Allies. The minds of most pacifists on this continent have been so conditioned during the past two decades that the mere thought of war paralyses them and renders them incapable of passing rational judgment on the facts of the present situation. Thus they cannot, or will not, realize that the revolutionary Nazi movement, which suppresses freedom by terror and moulds the youth of the world by

pagan propaganda until Christianity and individual liberty
are despised, is not prepared to leave us in peace. Its
gospel, as Hitler has said, can endure no rival and must
exterminate all other faiths—and yet it is in itself rather a
nihilistic suppression of all the higher and gentler qualities
of religion and life. If it were merely a matter of the
political domination of the world by Germany, a case
might be made for the ultimate spiritual victory of a
Christendom that surrendered to it only to leaven it, a
spiritual counterpart of Horace's *Graecia capta ferum
victorem cepit;* but the aggressor is not Germany but
Naziism, a force that seeks to mould human minds and
spirits to its own image. Christendom may well refuse
to surrender its children's souls and its terrestrial existence
to a régime of atheistic suppression.

Resistance to this nihilistic movement can thus form a
purpose common to thinking Canadians of all religious
faiths and all racial origins. To think our national way
through to the true meaning of the present menace in all
countries, will be to provide a high unity of resolve.

At the same time, it is imperative that we discriminate
between Naziism and its first victim, the German nation.
Let us remember the details of Hitler's seizure of power in
1933—how after his Brown-shirt gangster-brigades had
wiped out all rival parties, murdered hundreds of their
leaders, burned the Reichstag building to give colour to the
story of an impending Communist revolution, and terrorized the polling-booths throughout Germany, the Nazis
still received only 43 per cent. of the total vote, and it was
only in a Reichstag terrorized by armed Storm Troopers
that the bill giving him dictatorial powers was at last
rammed through. Naziism is our enemy, and not the
German people.

In this matter, indiscriminate intolerance on the Allied side might well prove fatal in the international field. Many zealous Anglo-Canadians, intoxicated with a sincere sense of the justice of our cause, simply do not realize the appallingly serious task with which we are confronted and the very real possibility of disaster that lies ahead. In Germany today there is a dominant Nazi minority, which has led the nation into war; there is also a strong Communist minority, into whose hands a revolution, promptly backed by Stalin, might easily transfer mastery; and in between lies the cowed bulk of the German people, who tolerate Hitler's régime lest a worse fate befall them. Hitler's unprincipled gangsterism is becoming increasingly evident to his own people, especially since his alliance with Stalin. Therein lies the main hope of the British psychological attack. If, in our folly, however, we declare war on the German nation as such, and talk wildly and irresponsibly about the necessity of permanently dismembering the Reich, or placing it under a British garrison, we shall nerve the whole German nation to a frenzied, and perhaps successful, unity of resistance. It is indicative of impressions already acquired to that effect, that Pastor Niemöller, from his concentration camp martyrdom, has already volunteered (thus far in vain) to fight in the submarine division of the German navy. With the elimination of Poland, moreover, and the neutrality of Russia, Italy, Belgium, and the United States, our armies face a more desperate issue than at any time during the World War. In that struggle, we won because the German nation at last believed that we discriminated between them and Caesarism, and intended a just peace. How can we expect to win this time, in the face of far greater odds, if we convince them from the very beginning that we plan

an intolerant suppression of their nationhood? Any
Canadian, therefore, who thus gives way to animosity
against the entire German people, is gratifying his spleen
at the expense of his brains, and is helping to ensure
Canada's defeat in war.

Even if we should win the war, however, in spite of a
widespread spirit of hatred towards the German nation,
we should infallibly lose the peace. In our inevitable
spirit of vindictiveness, we should find ourselves emo-
tionally and mentally incapable of framing a peace that
would survive. Even more tragic than defeat in this war,
would be the establishment after victory of a world system
whose inevitable collapse in bloodshed would render all our
sacrifices in vain.

In order, therefore, that we may keep clear to ourselves,
to the German people, and to nations now neutral, the
ends for which we are prepared to die, it is imperative that
we should plan and make public the peace we purpose.
The past failure of the League of Nations does not mean
that collective security is an impossible ideal, but rather that
its earlier plan was too timid and that the forces of national
selfishness were too strong. Unless, however, human intelligence is incapable of profiting by the errors of the past,
we should be able—if a second chance, after this dark
struggle, is vouchsafed to us—to build an enduring world
order with wiser minds and surer hands. But we must
plan now. It will be fatal to wait to improvise in the tense
atmosphere of an armistice. Our hopes for the war and
for the peace are in a large measure dependent on an early
clarification of our political philosophy and programme.

A complete set of blue-prints for the constructive task
after the war is beyond the scope of the present volume.
The following suggestions are set down as major points to

be considered by the architects of the better world for which we hope:

1. The peace will need to be one of constructive collaboration, and not a dictated peace imposed punitively by the victors on the vanquished. At the present moment, that free and pacific collaboration is impossible, not only because the gross and continual mendacity of Herr Hitler makes it unthinkable that any nation can rely upon his word, but also because his proposed terms involve our acceptance of unrighteous violence in the permanent subjugation of non-Germanic peoples. We must therefore seek to envisage his replacement by another German government, with which we can discuss, in amity and confidence, the reconstruction of Europe and the world.

2. The primary prerequisite of that new world will be an effective federalism of all civilized states that are prepared to abide by the terms of federation. So long as national sovereignty is insisted on in its starkest and most categorical sense, there can be no solution to Europe's political problems and we shall go on from catastrophe to catastrophe, generation after generation. The forces of unmitigated nationalism, impelling linguistic groups, both large and small, to achieve statehood in a world where their living space will always infringe on the living space of others and where their attempts to achieve unity and security by the repression of minority rights will perpetuate hatreds internally and externally, will make world peace impossible unless their economic and political problems can be pooled in a vaster federal system. In such a system, on the other hand, with security for the component units no longer a grave problem, the fullest freedom for minority cultures, regardless of frontiers, becomes a peaceful possibility. There is a sense in which

political sovereignty has ceased to be possible, when the aggressive preparations of a nation like Germany can force the most drastic and costly changes on a score of other countries. The calamitous cost of national defence, coupled with the ruin of normal world trade in an endeavour to achieve autarky in case of war, must compel even the most fanatical nationalist to face the federal solution. When the alternative to federalism is bankruptcy, wholesale extermination, and the progressive collapse of civilization, an abatement of sovereignty even by the largest states seems a small price to pay for survival. Even at that, there would not need to be any change in the political structure of the federal states. Republics and kingdoms could still exist side by side.

3. There should be an effective federal government, with specified fields of authority. Representation should be in proportion to population, as in the United States of America.

4. A bold solution to vast economic problems would need to be met in a spirit of mutual sacrifice. Among these issues which would not be insoluble if the will to solve them were present would be (a) a *Zollverein*, or customs union, to open the clogged channels of trade; (b) a common currency; (c) a rationalization of agriculture and industry, in terms of regional resources and skills. The third of these problems, with its reversal of the artificial freeze-up of economics through autarkic war policies, would, to a large extent, solve itself if the first two problems could be settled over a large enough area. The problem of raw materials as between have and have-not countries would also be automatically solved.

5. There should be a single federal army for police duty and foreign defence. Armaments should be reduced to a level adequate for these tasks. All private munitions

companies should be expropriated and all munitions works placed under the control of the federal government.

6. Civil and religious liberty should be guaranteed by the federal authority. Inasmuch as the chief threat to such liberty in our times comes from organized revolutionary groups of the Right and Left, the formation of private armies of the Storm Trooper type should be prohibited. No arrogant "self-conscious minority" of either extreme should be permitted to impose a despotism by direct action. In political liberty itself there is scope for the rational, gradual outworking of necessary changes in our social structure.

7. While colonies should be developed, under federal trusteeship, for the benefit of the native peoples, steps should be taken to secure equality of access to their resources for all members of the federal system.

8. The re-establishment of an ethnic Polish state and an ethnic Czech state would be necessary guarantees of German sincerity. Areas indubitably Polish (thus including Poznania and Pomorze) and Czech (most of Bohemia-Moravia) should have full autonomy within the federal system. A general Danubian settlement, in which Czech and Rumanian violence and intrigue twenty years ago prevented plebiscites and produced the preposterous frontiers of Trianon, should be subject to self-determination on the part of the populations concerned. Austria, likewise, should have the right of independent choice, as against dictation either from Germany *or from the Allies*. Her decision, granted civil and religious liberty, freed from the Nazi terror, would probably be in favour of membership in a confederation of German states.

The League of Nations was an instrument of international security that failed because the nations never had

the moral courage to use it. It was a beneficent spirit that
remained disembodied. The new proposal would seek the
effective incarnation of that League spirit in an actual
federation of as many states as could realize its necessity.
In the active propagation of such a policy, Canada can
harmonize her highest national interest with the highest
interests of mankind.

When we turn from foreign to domestic policy in
Canada today, we shall need to realize that liberty is something whose perpetuation in Canada will call for more
patriotism, justice, and sacrifice than we have been ready
to concede in the past. The main challenge of the totalitarian states is not the military challenge, serious as that
is, but the challenge created when our people see, or think
that they see, in Germany, in Russia, or in Italy, a solution of the problems that plague our own national life.
Seen from a distance and through a mist of class prejudice
or economic malaise, the idealistic side of the totalitarian
achievement will be seen to the exclusion of its grievous
losses. Nay more, the advocates of the new gospel will
insist that democracy, after an incompetent and helpless
life, is now dead, and that national prosperity and national greatness are only possible under highly organized
and despotic leadership.

What is the answer to these feverish movements that
would stifle liberty, allegedly in the name of justice and in
the interest of the nation? The answer is that we must so
set our house in order, economically, politically, and
socially, that there will be no excuse for revolution.
Fascism and Communism are fevers against which a
healthy community is immune by nature. But so long as
there is misery and injustice, there will also be grave
danger of infection. It is irrational for us to preach on the

one hand the message of more abundant life for men, and at the same time to take no urgent interest in the removal of the slums, the stagnant pools of unused labour, and the futile currents of transient labour-hawking, out of which lives of wretchedness and vice and frustration must inevitably come.

The price of liberty for ourselves and our children need not necessarily be martyrdom. It is rather the more difficult and exacting task of applying Christian zeal and Christian intelligence to the solution of our social and economic problems, to removing the animosities that embitter group with group and race with race, and to making it possible for men, women, and children to live wholesome, industrious, well-rounded lives. It needs to be demonstrated to those who praise the iron efficiency of absolutism, that a liberal democracy can also meet the demands of social justice and at the same time safeguard the values of individual personality. A benevolent dictatorship has no restraints to keep it from going sour, and becoming a thing of selfish cruelty, evil, and horror. Liberal democracy, on the contrary, is self-cleansing through its very freedom of thought and discussion. Its weakness lies in its tendency to talk instead of act, while selfish interests exploit their privileges and institutions for gain-seeking ends. But with devoted leadership, imagination, and constructive power, there is no reason why our free institutions should not transform our world into something finer and fairer.

Into that pattern of a higher civilization, based on domestic justice and playing an honourable part in the evolution of world federalism, our Canadian minority cultures could be fitted with far greater ease and profit. At the present time, there is danger of these minority

groups being regarded as a threat to national unity by
reason of their very diversity of experience and tradition;
but in a world where European crusades for national
sovereignty and living space need no longer cause heart-
burnings and animosities among ex-nationals here in
Canada, it would be easier to institute policies of liberalism
towards the languages and cultures of all our citizens.

These ideal circumstances are, of course, still in the
future. In the year of grace 1939, a survey of Canada's
two and a half million citizens of European origin (other
than English and French), as revealed in their vernacular
press, shows potent and antagonistic forces at work.
Among the Russians, Ukrainians, Finns, and Hungarians,
there are active and astute Communist groups, who, in
identical terms, have long been vociferously denouncing
Germany and demanding a military alliance of the Western democracies with "the greatest democracy of all",
Soviet Russia. Among the Germans, Italians, and Ukrainians, there have been equally vocal Fascist groups, violently denouncing both Communism and democracy, and
representing British foreign policy as consistently weak
and evil. The Russo-German pact of August 1939, apparently the result of long secret negotiation, makes one
question the sincerity of both their inspired presses in
Canada, and suspect them equally as menaces to the
fundamental interests of the Dominion. Nevertheless, the
great majority of the European-Canadians, of all origins,
belong to neither of these extreme camps, but are more or
less democratic in their outlook. Furthermore, almost all
of our European-Canadians except the Communists have
strong ties of affection for the respective countries of their
origin and intense interest in political developments there.
In the case of the Ukrainian nationalists, the Zionist Jews,

and the extremer German and Italian nationalists, Canada
has tended to serve as an actual base for political activities
directed from abroad. The Hungarians, Czechs, Poles, and
Croats, while not thus actively political, are profoundly
moved as to the fates of their national brothers in Europe.
Even the Dutch and the Scandinavians abound in organizations to preserve a cultural contact with the countries from which they sprang. Our fifty national minorities,
great and small, inherit an allegiance of affection for fifty
different motherlands.

To some Canadian nationalists whom I have met, such a
situation is a matter for immediate protest. The Anglo-
Canadian in particular, distrustful of what he does not
understand, feels that it is imperative at all costs to transform all these other nationals into Anglo-Saxons. Under
war-time conditions especially, it is to be feared that there
will be a sharp increase of intolerance on the part of the
Anglo-Canadians and a greater insistence on "assimilat-
ing" all minorities with the utmost rigour. There are
already increasing signs of Fascism in the Dominion, and
that is a temper which would seek, as in Germany, to
obliterate all minority rights in the name of national
unity. In other words, it would seek, not merely to make
good Canadians of our Magyars, Scandinavians, Germans,
and Slavs, but actually, by some mysterious chemical action under high pressure, to transmute them into English-
men. During the Great War, summary action of this
sort, in abolishing bilingual schools in Western Canada,
alienated many citizens even in groups like the Icelanders,
who had surpassed the native Anglo-Canadians in vol-
untary enlistment.

What should be Canada's attitude towards the group
activities of her minorities? Before answering that

question, let us remind ourselves of the present trend in
Canadian population. The British-Canadians are at last
less than half of the country's total and are losing ground
at an alarming rate. "Blessed are the child-bearers" is the
primary beatitude of sociology; but the Anglo-Canadians
(and especially the Protestant portion, with whom religious sanctions are no longer strong enough to ensure
that normal average family of four which is statistically
necessary for the survival of a race or a group) are apparently destined, as a mere matter of simple arithmetic,
to dwindle in the course of a century to a negligible frac-
tion of the whole. In such circumstances, it would be
dubious wisdom to indulge in any policies of compulsion
that might savour of injustice. It has been the fashion
since 1918 to denounce pre-War Austria and Hungary for
their stress on the German and Magyar languages in
education and official life, but the United States and the
English provinces of Canada have been scarcely less rigorous in their insistence on English. I am not arguing for the
extension of the number of Canada's official languages;
for that way, confusion would lie. Even the Czechs, after
nearly a century of agitation against the use of German as
Austria's *Amtsprache*, found that they had to insist on
Czech as the one official language for all the six language-
groups of Czechoslovakia. But there might be wisdom in
a hospitable attitude towards a study of the languages and
cultures of our minorities. Exposed as we constantly are
to a great ocean of American English through press and
radio, there would be small danger to our national unity
even in bilingual schools of the type sanctioned in Manitoba from 1897 to 1916; and there would be a counter-
vailing element of good will towards a country that did
not obviously seek to stamp out the citizen's mother

tongue in addition to imparting an essential knowledge of English.

All the values of civilization are not summed up in the Anglo-Saxon. To weave into the Canadian fabric the multicoloured threads of all of Europe's cultural legacies ought, if it were possible, to produce in the end a civilization of unusual richness. In the ancient Greek world, it was Athens, the most miscegenated in blood and culture, that led in all artistic and cultural achievements, while Sparta, which kept its Nordic stock relatively pure, was left far behind in everything except the art of war.

For the individual, moreover, a process whereby he is cut off entirely from his cultural and linguistic past and made an orphan in an alien land is not likely to produce the happiest results. A man is likely to become a better Canadian, and to make a more confident and valuable contribution to Canadian life, if he is led to feel pride in his own national past and to realize that his fellow-Canadians, because they admire and respect his national tradition, expect great things from him. On the other hand, he is under a psychological handicap of bitterness or humiliation if he is regarded as belonging to "lesser breeds without the Law" and only permitted to share in the life of the Chosen People on the condition, compulsorily applied, that he renounce his own people and all that they have stood for.

If this principle be valid, Canada ought to welcome all those minority organizations of a non-political character that help the individual to cherish his cultural past and to mobilize its resources for his more effective participation in Canadian life. Excellent examples are the League of Norsemen in Canada, the Icelandic National League, the Associated Poles, the Federation of Polish Societies in

Canada, the Institute Prosvita, the Roma Society, and the Deutsch-Kanadische Verband. To such organizations as these, it would be desirable to give every sort of encouragement, including sincere evidence of friendly regard, both personal and official, from members of the Anglo-Canadian community. Among their own groups, they are as legitimate as the St. Andrew's Society among the Canadian Scotch; and their love of their language is as natural as that which has just created a Gaelic college in Cape Breton.

On the other hand, minority organizations with a militantly political character, especially those organized by agents of foreign powers, owing allegiance to foreign governments, or perpetuating old hatreds alien to Canadian life, should be subject to grave disapprobation. Such, for example, are the "Sitch" Guards of the Ukrainian Nationalist Organization, organized by Colonel Roman Shushko, director of the Ukrainian revolutionary headquarters (O.U.N.) in Berlin, as a feeder to his European machine. Similar, too, are the Deutsche Bund, the Deutsche Arbeitsfront, the Canadian branch of the Nazi party, and the Canadian branch of the Italian Fascist party, all of which are directly under the orders of European governments.

While viewing these forms of political interference with hostility, and the more purely cultural activities of patriotic European-Canadians with a discriminating cordiality, the Anglo-Canadian can nevertheless scarcely view with equanimity the rapid replacement of his own stock by that of alien groups. The Anglo-Saxons, who have displayed the greatest political genius of any age or people, have bequeathed to Canada the master-principles of responsible representative government and of federalism. As heirs of that tradition and still the largest of the many national groups in Canada, the Anglo-Canadians naturally hope for the perpetuation of their blood and institutions in this land. For the former, our Anglo-Canadian birth-rate is no longer adequate, and immigration from the British Isles (where the birth-rate is still lower) has been relatively unsuccessful since the War. Unless we are prepared to take parenthood as a serious duty, *la revanche du berceau* will speedily submerge us in both East and West—and that deservedly, when the potential mothers of our race mistake comfort for civilization.

Whether or not our younger married generation reconsecrates itself to its marital duty, the problem of perpetuating our institutions remains. It is important that we should seek once more to make democratic liberalism a living and vital thing. Revolutionary ideologies of the Right and Left are tireless amongst us in their propagation of tyrannic faiths, each seeking in the name of a self-conscious minority to fasten the shackles of a doctrinaire system upon the indifferent majority. Democratic liberalism stands for no such intolerant compulsion. Its aim is the fullest and richest development of every individual, and that development is only possible in an atmosphere of civil and religious liberty. It is the individual and not the state that counts. Given basic economic and social justice for all, the political forms of the state can be freely adjusted to meet human needs in a system of parliamentary liberty. Only thus can we escape the despotism of doctrinaire rigidity in a revolutionary state, and move at a level to which the revolutionary theorist, obsessed with man as a mere economic animal, rarely rises. Man is superior to the beast only in those aspects of his life which are superior to the animal functions of eating, drinking, working, playing, and sleeping. And in that higher world of music, art, literature, and religious faith, the essential conditions are those of personal freedom, rather than the suffocating mental dungeon of a police state under a totalitarian régime.

The gospel of freedom should therefore have a positive rather than a passive place in our Canadian national life. Revolutionary ideologies sweep across all frontiers today with their strident assurance to eager young men that action is the all-necessary factor in life. It is essential that we shall show young Canadians rather that while it is far easier to destroy than to achieve, the only sure warrant of progress and permanence will lie in the sober counsels of reasonable men tested in the open sunlight of free discussion. Too long we have taken our liberal democracy for granted. Today we must exalt it as a high and vital reality—no dead doctrinaire theory but the only soil in which full human character can grow, the only air that can permanently sustain life in the free institutions of Canada or in that ampler world of international peace and federalism for which we strive beyond the war.

BIBLIOGRAPHY

ASZTALOS, MIKLOS, *A történeti Erdély* (Budapest, 1936).
BAERLEIN, H., *The Birth of Yugoslavia* (London, 1922).
BALLA, VALENTINE DE, *The New Balance of Power in Europe* (Baltimore, 1932).
BENES, EDWARD, *The Problems of Czechoslovakia* (Prague, 1936).
BETHLEN, COUNT S., *The Treaty of Trianon and European Peace* (London, 1928).
BORKENAU, F., *Austria and After* (London, 1938).
————, *The New German Empire* (London, 1939).
BRAUN, ROBERT, *Magyarország feldarabolása és a nemzetiségi kérdés* (Budapest, 1919).
BRENNECKE, FRITZ, *Vom deutschen Volk und seinem Lebensraum* (Munich, 1937).
BUELL, R. L., *Poland, the Key to Europe* (New York and London, 1939).
CHMELAR, JOSEF, *The German Problem in Czechoslovakia* (Prague, 1936).
CRABITES, PIERRE, *Beneš, Statesman of Central Europe* (London, 1935).
CRANE, J. O., *The Little Entente* (New York, 1931).
CSAKO, STEPHEN, *The Hungarian Problem* (Budapest, 1934).
DAMI, ALDO, *Les nouveaux martyrs: destin des minorités* (Paris, 1936).
DUTCH, O., *Thus died Austria* (London, 1938).
DYBOSKI, ROMAN, *Poland* (London, 1933).
ECKHART, FERENC, *Introduction à l'histoire hongroise* (Paris, 1928).
————, *A Short History of the Hungarian People* (London, 1931).
EINZIG, P., *Bloodless Invasion* (London, 1938).
ELEKES, DEZSO, *A dunavölgyi kérdőjel* (Budapest, 1934).
FLACHBARTH, ERNO, *Ruszinszkó autonómiája* (Miskolc, 1934).
FODOR, M. W., *South of Hitler* (London, 1938).
GARRATT, G. T., *Mussolini's Roman Empire* (London, 1938).
GEDYE, G. E. R., *Heirs to the Hapsburgs* (London, 1935).
GORECKI, ROMAN, *Poland and Her Economic Development* (London, 1935).

GOWER, SIR ROBERT, *The Hungarian Minorities in the Succession States* (London, 1937).
GRANT-DUFF, S., *German and Czech* (London, 1937).
————, *Europe and the Czechs* (London, 1938).
HALL, D. J., *Rumanian Furrow* (London, 1933).
HITLER, ADOLF, *Mein Kampf*, 311th edition (Berlin, 1938).
HOCH, CHARLES, *The Political Parties in Czechoslovakia* (Prague, 1936).
HOLLOS, ETIENNE, *Les modes charactéristiques et les types principaux de l'assimilation nationale* (Paris, 1937).
HORVATH, PROF. EUGENE, *Transylvania and the History of the Rumanians* (Budapest, 1935).
HURD, W. B., *Racial Origins and Nativity of the Canadian People* (Ottawa, 1938).
JASZI, O., *The Dissolution of the Habsburg Monarchy* (Chicago, 1929).
JEHLICKA, FRANCIS, *André Hlinka à la conference de la Paix de Paris* (Geneva, 1938).
————, *Father Hlinka's Struggle for Slovak Freedom* (London, 1938).
JEZIORANSKI, KONSTANTY, *National Minorities in Europe* (Warsaw, 1933).
KAAS, ALBERT AND LAZAROVICS, FEDOR, *Bolshevism in Hungary, the Béla Kún Period* (London, 1931).
KNIEZSA, ISTVAN, *A Szlávok* (Budapest, 1932).
KRISZTICS, SANDOR, *A békeszerződések reviziója* (Budapest, 1927).
KROFTA, KAMIL, *A Short History of Czechoslovakia* (London, 1935).
————, *Czechoslovakia and the Crisis of Collective Security* (Prague, 1936).
————, *Europe at the Cross-roads* (Prague, 1936).
LEHMANN, HEINZ, *Das Deutschtum in Ostkanada* (Stuttgart, 1931).
————, *Das Deutschtum in Westkanada* (Berlin, 1939).
LORIMER, E. O., *What Hitler Wants* (London, 1939).
LYPACEWICZ, WACLAW, *Polish-Czech Relations* (Warsaw, 1936).
MACARTNEY, C. A., *Social Revolution in Austria* (London, 1926).
————, *National States and National Minorities* (London, 1934).
————, *Hungary* (London, 1934).
————, *Hungary and her Successors* (London, 1937).
MACHRAY, R., *The Poland of Pilsudski* (London, 1936).
MACKAY, R. A. and ROGERS, E. B., *Canada Looks Abroad* (Toronto, 1938).

MALYUSZ, ELEMER, *The Fugitive Bolsheviks* (London, 1931).

MORAVEC, COL. EMANUEL, *The Strategic Importance of Czecho-slovakia for Western Europe* (Prague, 1936).

MORROW, I. F. D., *The Peace Settlement in the German-Polish Borderlands* (London, 1936).

NAGY, IVAN, *Les Hongrois dans le monde* (Pecs, 1938).

OTTER, SIR WILLIAM, *Internment Operations (Canada), 1914-1920* (Ottawa, 1921).

PAPOUSEK, JAROSLAV, *Czechoslovakia, Soviet Russia, and Germany* (Prague, 1936).

PAPROCKI, S. J., *Minority Affairs and Poland* (Warsaw, 1935: Nationality Research Institute).

PASVOLSKY, L., *Economic Nationalism of the Danubian States* (New York, 1928).

PATTERSON, E. J., *Yugoslavia* (London, 1936).

RIPLEY, W. Z., *The Races of Europe* (New York, 1923).

ROSE, W. J., *The Drama of Upper Silesia* (London, 1936).

——————, *Poland* (London, 1939).

SCHACHER, GERHARD, *Central Europe and the Western World* (London, 1936).

SCOTT, F. R., *Canada Today* (Toronto, 1938).

SCRIMALI, ANTONIO, *La regione autonoma della Rutenia dopo il trattato di San Germano* (Palermo, 1938).

SETON-WATSON, R. W., *Racial Problems in Hungary* (London, 1908).

——————, *The Southern Slav Question and the Habsburg Monarchy* (London, 1911).

——————, *A History of the Rumanians, from Roman times to the completion of unity* (London, 1934).

——————, *Britain and the Dictators* (London, 1938).

SMOGORZEWSKI, CASIMIR, *Poland's Access to the Sea* (London, 1934).

SZASZ, ZSOMBOR, *Románia* (Budapest, 1931).

STEED, H. WICKHAM, *The Doom of the Hapsburgs* (London, 1937).

TARJAN, EDMUND, and FALL, A., *Hungarians, Slovaks and Ruthenians in the Danube Valley* (Budapest, 1938).

TELEKI, COUNT PAUL, *The Evolution of Hungary and its Place in European History* (New York, 1923).

TELEKI, COUNT PAUL, *Les charactères régionaux de la Hongrie géographique* (Liége, 1926).

TEMPERLEY, H. W. V., *A History of Serbia* (London, 1919).

TILTMAN, H. HESSELL, *Peasant Europe* (London, 1934).

Tomas, Adam, *The 'Polish Corridor' and Peace* (Warsaw, 1930).
Toynbee, A. J., *Survey of International Affairs, 1920-3, 1924, etc.*, annual (London: Royal Institute of International Affairs).
Wiskemann, Elizabeth, *Czechs and Germans* (London, 1938).
Young, Chas. H., *The Ukrainian Canadians* (Toronto, 1931).
Zagoni, Istvan, *Wie in Rumänien ein Nationalitätstatut zustande kam* (Budapest, 1938).

General Reference

The Baltic States: Estonia, Latvia, Lithuania (London, 1938).
South-eastern Europe: A Political and Economic Survey (London, 1939).
Soviet Union Year Book (London).
Handbook of Central and East Europe (Zurich).
Year-Book of the Czechoslovak Republic (Prague).
Concise Statistical Year-Book of Poland (Warsaw).
Statesman's Year-Book (London).

Periodicals

Slavonic and East European Review (London).
International Affairs (London).
Bulletin of International Affairs (London).
Foreign Affairs (New York).

INDEX

AALAND ISLANDS, 101-2.
Albanian, 14, 73, 103.
Albanian-Canadians, 187.
Alberta Herold, 128-9, 187.
Alpine race, 12 *et seq.*
Anglo-Canadians, 107-111, 117, 203-4.
Anti-Comintern bloc, 34, 63, 92.
Anti-Semitism, 122-3, 142, 147, 159-161.
Arrow-Cross movement, 5.
Aryan, 10-11, 14, 15.
Associated Poles of Canada, 161, 202.
Athens, 16, 202.
Aufbau, Der, 129.
Austria, 6, 7, 13, 24, 25, 38, 102, 196, 201.

BALKANS, 32, 67-73.
Baltic States, 26, 33, 94-98.
Basque, 14, 18, 24, 25.
Belgian-Canadians, 187.
Belgium, 5, 14, 26, 99-100.
Bessarabia, 70, 75, 87.
Bilingual schools, 124, 201.
"Blue-shirts", 108, 190.
Bohemia-Moravia, 7, 25, 37, 40-43, 53, 196.
Bollettino Italo-Canadese, 166-171.
Bote, Der, 129-133.
Brest-Litovsk, Treaty of, 32, 80.
Breton, 14, 24.
Brody, Andrew, 50, 88.
Buduchnist Natsiyi, 146-7.
Bukovina, 70, 75, 87.
Bulgarian, 14, 27, 71.
Bulgarian-Canadians, 187.

CANADA, 5, 25, 105-205.
Canada Posten, 155.
Canada-Tidningen, 155.
Canadian Jewish Chronicle, 158-9.
Canadian Jewish Review, 158.
Canadian Orthodox Messenger, 149.
Canadian Union of Fascists, 169.

Carol, King, 70.
Carpatho-Russian Union, 50-53.
Carpatho-Ruthenia ("Carpatho-Ukraine"), 48-54, 75, 77, 87-9, 138, 139.
Catalan, 14, 24.
Catholic Church in Canada, 110, 111-4, 119-120, 129, 133-4, 146-7, 152, 161-3, 165-7, 180-182.
Češke Noviny, 187.
Cieszyn (Teschen), 38, 40, 41.
Colonies, 8, 30, 36-7, 196.
Communists in Canada, 147-8, 152, 158, 171-5, 176, 179-86, 190, 197.
Concentration Camps, 6, 111, 119, 149, 163.
Corridor (Pomorze), 7, 58-61.
Courier, Der, 120-1, 135.
Croat, Croatia, 14, 24-26, 39, 67-9.
Croatian-Canadians, 185-6, 200.
Czech-Canadians, 187, 200.
Czechs, Czechoslovakia, 5, 6, 8, 14, 24-28, 34, 38-54, 87-9, 102, 196, 201.

DANES, 24-6, 101-2.
Danish-Canadians, 153-5.
Danske Herold, 155.
Danzig, 7, 58-61.
Deutsche Arbeitsfront, 108, 128, 203.
Deutsche Ausland-Institut, 17, 129.
Deutsche Bund, 18, 108, 127-8, 132, 161, 203.
Deutsche Zeitung fuer Canada, 122-8, 160.
Deutsch-Kanadische Verband, 203.
Doukhobors, 171-6.
Dutch-Canadians, 186, 200.

EASTERN GALICIA, 25, 29, 75 *et seq.*, 84, 88, 137.
Estonia, 14, 24, 25, 32, 33, 94-8.
Estonian-Canadians, 187.
Ethiopia, 103.
European-Canadians, 116-188.